CONTEMPORARY AMERICAN LITERATURE : 1945–1972

CONTEMPORARY
AMERICAN
LITERATURE
1945-1972

AN INTRODUCTION

IHAB HASSAN

FREDERICK UNGAR PUBLISHING CO.

NEW YORK

COPYRIGHT © 1973 BY FREDERICK UNGAR PUBLISHING CO., INC.

PRINTED IN THE UNITED STATES OF AMERICA

LIBRARY OF CONGRESS CATALOG CARD NUMBER: 72–81701

ISBN: 0–8044–3121–3 (CLOTH)

0–8044–6248–8 (PAPER)

ACKNOWLEDGMENTS

I wish to thank the University of Wisconsin–Milwaukee and the Vilas Trust Fund for providing me with summer grants as well as honoring me with the research professorship that made this work possible. To the State of Wisconsin itself, as place and people, also my appreciation.

PREFACE

I intend this book, modestly and briefly, as an introduction to contemporary American literature. It may serve, coincidentally, as a work of reference, though it makes no claim of completeness. It may also provide a critical sense of the literature in question, though its mood is mainly presentational. But what is contemporary? I have simply applied this term to the period between 1945 and 1972. The writers included here all begin to publish during or after World War II. Almost all of them are born after the year 1910, which I have chosen as a plausible cut-off point. A few authors—too important to ignore, too old to discuss as an integral part of the postwar scene—I have labeled transitional.

The organization of the book is obvious. A general introduction limns the character of the period, which is also reflected in its non-fiction and criticism. Chapters on fiction, poetry, and drama then follow. Each chapter begins with a short introduction, moving from portraits of major and prominent authors, in chronological sequence, to glimpses of significant types and trends. These last are at best provisional categories, critical abstractions, balanced by the concrete reality of each individual talent. Since no end to a live and continuing effort can be envisioned, a chapter entitled "Without Conclusion" projects some of the most recent tendencies of the literary imagination into the near future. The final section contains a selective bibliography of works about contemporary American literature.

Some, no doubt, will question my choices, particularly those designated as "major" figures. This, the classic problem of every literary history, is troublesome in contemporary context; for the stature of an author may itself be a quality of retrospection. Still, the energy, scope, and centrality of some writers may permit us to single them out over the last three decades; their works seem to give the era its literary authority. In the end, however, the question of major figures may prove less premature than obsolete.

I should finally note that the book is written consciously in the present tense, which, though it may strike some readers as obtrusive, can still help to remind us of the demands of change.

I. H.

Milwaukee, Wisconsin
June 1972

CONTENTS

I

GENERAL INTRODUCTION

American literature bursts on the international scene in the early decades of the twentieth century. An epoch that includes T. S. Eliot, Ezra Pound, Robert Frost, William Carlos Williams, Wallace Stevens, Gertrude Stein, Sherwood Anderson, Ernest Hemingway, William Faulkner, F. Scott Fitzgerald, John Dos Passos, and Eugene O'Neill can hardly escape notice. The creative energy of these writers illumines the past anew; thus the old masters, from James Fenimore Cooper to Henry James, emerge in deeper perspective. Certain themes of the American imagination also begin to acquire richer hues: Innocence and Experience, Eden and Utopia, Self and Society, Nature and History. The symbolist and expressionist modes dominate poetry and drama; mock romance and autobiography prevail in fiction. Violent or sentimental, driven toward extremes of perception, struggling with history (Time) even more than with the frontier (Space), American literature develops a complete myth of itself against which every author feels that he must assert his own identity.

1

The identity of the American writers who establish themselves after World War II is collectively as well as individually distinct. These writers begin by dissociating themselves from both the literary and political inheritance of the Thirties, that is, from both naturalism and Marxism. For most of them, ideology requires too many simplifications in the forms of art; and the threat of totalitarianism, on the Left or on the Right, makes official views of reality suspect. The war itself, which absorbs much of their human energy, also gives them unflinching clarity, insight into their existence, and a prevision of things to come. Whatever illusions they retain after the war, these seem necessary to their survival; whatever techniques of literary evasion or assault they invent, further the same end.

Survival appears indeed both the secret and paramount obsession of contemporary man. In America, particularly, where change changes at a dizzy rate, man rushes ever faster toward a destiny overcast with final questions. These questions do not only concern the Doomsday Bomb. Memories of holocausts from Auschwitz to Hiroshima, a succession of wars from Korea to Vietnam, the earth exploding in numbers, ravages to the natural environment, renewed awareness of poverty in America, the discriminations of race and sex, political protest of every kind—all these perpetuate a mood of crisis that no writer can entirely ignore. Science can capture the moon or alter the genes of mankind, but none knows how the ultimate moral and historical decisions can be made. Some think technology heroic, others viciously rampant, yet many agree that the collapse of older values leaves the world in the form of organized chaos, a demonic mixture of order and anarchy. A massive invasion of human privacy takes place as the media of control and of communication exchange their functions, as computers at once ease and complicate the patterns of social existence. Increasingly, the public realm seems ruled by a variety of fantasies, instantaneous, comical, dreadful. For the individual, violence, nihilism, *anomie* offer no genuine alternatives to the surrealism of mass society and the superstate. This experience, shared abroad, deepens the affinities between American and European literature, between nations witnessing the strange paradox of a world extensively homogenized yet intensely fragmented. It is as if Marshall McLuhan's prophecy of the Global Village—which refers both to the relentless encirclement of the earth through communication and the sharp withdrawal of its peoples into nations, sects, and tribes—were suddenly come true.

Yet despite the culture of the postwar era, curiously violent and hedonistic, angry and apathetic, the American writer makes a place for his imagination in it. If he can not escape the deep bemusement of his country—it amounts to a crisis of confidence in the "American way of life"—neither can he deny the enormous vitality that still throbs about him. Part of this energy sustains his creations, experiments, rebellions; he feels new languages and values taking hold in literature. His country searches continuously its brief past even as it incarnates the future of the world in the present; thus it compels him to live perilously at the point where prophecy and nostalgia meet. If the American dream often gives way to nightmare, the nightmare yields still to other dreams in the small hours of the dawn.

It were also an error to speak of the postwar period as if it possessed a unified character. Each decade witnesses shifts in personal tone as in public policy. This is perhaps most obvious in the symbolic turns of the Presidency. When Roosevelt dies in 1945, the explosion at Hiroshima has not yet taken place; mankind is still some small way from the Atomic Age. Truman makes the fateful decision and sees the war to a close; the Marshall Plan begins to link and restore broken nations. The fervency of the late Forties, induced not only by the sense of justified victory, nor only by the rise of

America into clear preeminence, expresses some hope in the possibilities of life at midcentury. But the Truman Doctrine soon certifies the realities of the Cold War; power politics begets caution, internal restraint. The reign of affluence *cum* conformity, broken sporadically by anti-Communist hysteria or Beatnik disaffiliation, follows in the Fifties during the Eisenhower years. Secretary Dulles's notion of Massive Retaliation hangs in the air while the Silent Generation, so called by the editors of *Time* and *Life*, founds its suburbias and its exurbias. With the inauguration of Kennedy in 1960, however, the country regains youthful consciousness of itself; it develops a style that befits its slogan, the New Frontier. But the assassination of Kennedy in 1963 seems to trigger a new kind of violence or insanity in the nation; the murderers of Martin Luther King and of Robert Kennedy strike in that same decade. Meanwhile, the Johnson Administration fails to create the Great Society; America sinks deeper into the Vietnam War, rending itself with dissent and division. The Berkeley Free Speech Movement of 1964 precedes rebellious forces of every kind: SDS and Weatherman; SNCC, CORE, and Black Panthers; Women's Lib and the Gay Liberation Front; Chicano and Red Power. During the Sixties, the counter culture of the Hippies and Yippies, Freaks and Crazies, thrives; dropouts and communes spread from Haight Ashbury to Staten Island; the interest in psychedelics and the occult crests; and the ecological movement, starting late, spreads everywhere. Though it is much too early to define the mood of the Seventies, a certain reaction against the frantic activism of the immediate past can be discerned under the Nixon Administration. It is as if the student killings at Kent State and Jackson State, and the massive protests against the invasion of Cambodia, all taking place in 1970, mark some turning point in the psychic life of America. President Nixon devalues the dollar, journeys to Peking and Moscow; the future remains unknown.

Yet the climate of ideas surrounding the American writer is far more dense, more diverse, than political slogans and events can indicate. Trends in sociology and psychology, philosophy and theology, science and technology also reveal the changing quality of the decades, reveal the facts and fantasies of the contemporary mind. These trends enrich the literary imagination even as they challenge it; and they suggest ways of reflecting reality that the public sometimes finds more arresting than the traditional poem, novel, or play. Hence the currency of non-fiction—sometimes called the "higher journalism"—and its increasing authority even among devoted students of literature. Hence, too, the relevance of certain academic disciplines and ideologies that help to formalize the hidden patterns of experience.

In the Fifties, ideas about culture seem particularly rife. Thus, for instance, David Riesman examines a new social trend, which he calls "other-direction," in his two influential works, *The Lonely Crowd* (1950) and *Individualism Reconsidered* (1954). The trend effects a subtle revision of American individualism and the Protestant work ethic, a revision of "inner-direction" and all its attendant values. Astute in his analysis of behavior, Riesman chooses not to judge it. His moral neutrality is shared by Alfred Kinsey in his two compendious and controversial works, *Sexual Behavior of the American Male* (1948) and *Sexual Behavior of the American Female* (1953). Based on statistics and personal interviews, these studies raise philosophic questions about the role of science in society, deny the concept of sexual "normality," and so challenge the romantic ideals of the nation. C. Wright Mill, on the other hand, challenges the American idea of democracy. In his two books, *White Collar* (1951) and *The Power Elite* (1956), Mill passionately exposes the invisible economic and political controls of a postindustrial nation. Different as they are in theme and method, all these works—and others, too, such as William H. Whyte's *The Organiza-*

tion Man (1956), Vance Packard's *The Hidden Persuaders* (1957), John Kenneth Galbraith's *The Affluent Society* (1958) —point to the emergence of a new social order. This new dispensation, sometimes helplessly called "mass society," is documented in such massive studies as Max Lerner's *America as a Civilization* (1957), such anthologies as Bernard Rosenberg's and David Manning White's *Mass Culture* (1957) or Eric Larrabee and Rolf Meyersohn's *Mass Leisure* (1958).

The general interest in anthropology and psychology also reaches a peak in the same decade. Though many anthropologists make major contributions before the war, some of their best works—such as Margaret Mead's *Coming of Age in Samoa* (1928) and Ruth Benedict's *Patterns of Culture* (1934)—achieve popularity only in the postwar industry of paperbacks. The literary awareness of myth, ritual, and archetype becomes acute in the Fifties, abetted by critics who expound the special relevancy of archaic form to modern artifice. Going back to such classics as Sigmund Freud's *Totem and Taboo* (1918) and James Frazer's *The Golden Bough* (1922), or to more recent translations of C. G. Jung's *Psychology and Alchemy* (1953) and Otto Rank's *The Myth of the Birth of the Hero* (1959), men of letters retrieve those fundamental images of nature and psyche, those primordial relations of man to his universe, that Eliot, Joyce, and Mann so richly exploited a generation earlier. In this perspective, such works as Joseph Campbell's *The Hero with a Thousand Faces* (1949) and Philip Wheelwright's *The Burning Fountain* (1954) prove of special interest to the mythographic critic.

Quite independently, psychoanalysis offers a new mode of discourse in urban America, creates its own kind of patter and intellectual orthodoxy. Yet, as Lionel Trilling brilliantly shows in *Freud and the Crisis of Our Culture* (1955), psychoanalysis also contains elements of a philosophy of art and of existence, the latter darkly articulated in Freud's own

Civilization and Its Discontents (1930). In literature, particularly, the ideas of character and action, dream and reality, symbol and metaphor, wit and humor, acquire new vitality from the theory of instincts; and man's ageless conflict with himself or others yields new cultural meanings. In time, the American psychoanalytic movement spreads to include the social psychology of Harry Stack Sullivan and Karen Horney, and the original thought of Erik Erikson, whose works, from *Childhood and Society* (1950) to *Identity: Youth and Crisis* (1968), command wide respect. Standing farthest away from Freudian psychoanalysis, B. F. Skinner develops his own experimental brand of psychology which he calls, after Pavlov and Watson, Behaviorism. In Skinner's view, Behaviorism aspires to nothing less than a complete science and technology of human behavior, predicting and controlling all actions. Though his ideas appear as early as the utopian novel *Walden Two* (1947), the full impact of his prophecy, terrifying to some and blissful to others, becomes evident only in *Beyond Freedom and Dignity* (1971).

In retrospect, the Fifties seem a decade of cultural implosion if not of gray-flanneled conformity. Yet the decade is not ruled exclusively by a corporate mystique; nor is it dominated only by the sociological imagination. Tough-minded and cogent, Reinhold Niebuhr calls for an active Christian faith in such works as *Christian Realism and Political Problems* (1953) and *The Self and the Dramas of History* (1955). The formal theologies of Karl Barth and Paul Tillich recreate the fundamental questions of Protestantism, and also renew religious discourse among the laity. Thus, for instance, Tillich's *The Courage to Be* (1952) makes its well-known case for religious existentialism. Thus, too, the names of Gabriel Marcel, Nicolas Berdyaev, Martin Buber, and Karl Jaspers become widely known. Their abundant thoughts, spanning various nationalities and faiths, appeal to Americans seeking new means of self-definition or self-transcendence. Indeed, the religious will of the Fifties implies more than self-transcendence; it implies sometimes a rejection of Western consciousness. This is dramatized by the Beat Movement and by the revivals of Oriental mysticism and Zen Buddhism in which D. T. Suzuki and Alan Watts play a significant part.

Yet opposition to the clichés of affluence and conformity in America can also draw on the secular resources of existentialism, on man's turbulent sense of the Self. There is much, after all, in the American experience that proves congenial to the existential view of man's nudity, his self-reliance, his defiance of mortality. Thus the ideas of Sartre and particularly of Camus take hold in native soil during the Fifties. These ideas are in fact preceded by the Hipster's way of life: close to danger and instinct and the rebellious imperative of his soul, the Hipster pits his whole being against the void of apocalypse. This portrait of the hero of the American night comes from Mailer's celebrated essay "The White Negro." The essay appears in *Advertisements for Myself* (1959), which seems to mark a turning point in the sensibility of the age.

If the Fifties appear implosive, the succeeding decade must be called explosive. The sociological, religious, and existential interests of the former years continue into the Sixties, though the temper of the times becomes more antinomian, more experimental. All is called into doubt; new styles of life evolve in every direction.

Something of this mood is reflected in the numerous works of Paul Goodman, from *Communitas* (1947), co-authored with Percival Goodman, through the signal works *Growing Up Absurd* (1960) and *Like a Conquered Province* (1967). Though Goodman's prose can sometimes be dreary, he is a versatile thinker, at ease in many disciplines. He qualifies his utopian drive with pragmatism, calling himself a "community anarchist," and tries to mediate between the Old Left and the New. His ideas on bureaucracy, "boondoggling,"

sexual liberty, national hypocrisy, radical politics, and especially education, find currency in the youth cultures of the
Sixties. Yet in the end, other works, such as Kenneth Ken-
niston's *The Young Radicals* (1968), Theodore Roszack's
The Making of a Counter Culture (1969), and Charles A.
Reich's *The Greening of America* (1970), may give a warmer
sense of the youth movements.

During the Sixties, the intellectual influences of Norman O.
Brown, Herbert Marcuse, Marshall McLuhan, and R. Buckminster Fuller also begin to be widely felt. In *Life against
Death* (1959), Brown initiates his radical psychoanalytic
critique of language, history, and the Freudian ego, a critique,
really, of that "disease called man." His project is the re-
covery of the life-instincts through a Dionysian consciousness.
In *Love's Body* (1966), a hieratic work written in aphorisms
of disturbing poetic intensity, Brown goes farther, calling for
the abolition of repressive culture and reason, of the reality
principle itself. His symbolic vision encompasses the lost
unity of all things. Though it is hard to convey the quality
of that original vision, its power touches the new body consciousness—the kind associated with Esalen Institute, say
—and appears to validate occultism, polymorphous perversity, mystic eroticism. In this, Brown stands in a line of
Freudian revisionists foreshadowed by Wilhelm Reich. Another line, that of existential psychoanalysis, foreshadowed
by Heidegger, Sartre, Jaspers, and Binswanger, leads to the
American work of Abraham Maslow and of Rollo May, whose
Love and Will (1969) enjoys considerable popularity.

The psychology of Herbert Marcuse, in *Eros and Civilization* (1955), shares some of Brown's early concerns, though
Marcuse's notion of "surplus repression," and indeed his
whole secular frame of mind, owe more to the dialectic
philosophy of Marx and Hegel than to Brown's tradition of
mythic and hermetic beliefs. It is mainly as a post-Marxist
prophet of revolution, as a contemporary Jeremiah denounc-

ing the "warfare-welfare state," that Marcuse becomes known
to radical movements around the world. In *One Dimensional
Man* (1964), *Critique of Pure Tolerance* (1967), and *An
Essay on Liberation* (1969), he invokes historical reason and
creative revolt, the transcendent powers of "negativity," to
combat "repressive tolerance" and the "total administration"
of existence. The connections are complex between Marcuse's
thought and such statements of the New Left as Michael
Harrington's *Toward a Democratic Left* (1968), Tom Hayden's *Rebellion and Repression* (1969), and, in a more antic
spirit, Free's (Abbie Hoffman) *Revolution for the Hell of It*
(1968) and Jerry Rubin's *Do It* (1970).

But the major challenge to the contemporary mind comes
from science and technology, which threaten to transform
man, society, and nature irreversibly. The breakthroughs of
science itself often go unnoticed by the public until a bomb
atomizes an atoll or a man takes a giant step on the moon;
yet everyone feels the implications of these breakthroughs
to be urgent. A number of books convey this sense of urgency,
miracle, and crisis, beginning with Norbert Wiener's *The
Human Use of Human Beings* (1950) and including such
current works as Gordon Rattray Taylor's *The Biological
Time Bomb* (1968), René Dubos's *So Human an Animal*
(1968), and Alvin Toffler's *Future Shock* (1970).

Among prophets of the new technology, Marshall Mc-
Luhan addresses himself to the impact of various media on
culture. His works, notably *The Gutenberg Galaxy* (1962),
Understanding Media (1964), *War and Peace in the Global
Village* (1968), and *Culture Is Our Business* (1970), scatter
brilliant and erratic insights into contemporary life, which,
as McLuhan says, we prefer to observe in a rear-view mirror.
Arguing that media are extensions of man, and that each
medium constitutes its own message, he contrasts the culture
of an earlier age (mechanical, linear, print-oriented, visual)
to the present culture (electric, non-linear, television-oriented,

audio-tactile). "As electrically contracted, the globe is no more than a village," he concludes. Following his own non-linear logic, he adopts in his later works a mode of representation using captions, collages, cartoons, quotations, jokes, and puns inspired by *Finnegans Wake*.

R. Buckminster Fuller goes still farther in applying the principles of his "comprehensive, anticipatory design science" to the human condition. Architect of the geodesic dome and of the dymaxion house, he is also a mathematician, cartographer, inventor, cosmogonist, and poet of the galactic age, insisting on man's harmonious existence, without scarcity or war, on this "spaceship earth." His works, including *Automation Education* (1962), *Nine Chains to the Moon* (1963), *Utopia or Oblivion* (1969), and *Operating Manual for Spaceship Earth* (1970), develop a recurrent pattern of benevolent ideas. These refer to man's mind as the "anti-entropic" force in creation; to the process of "ephemeralization," doing constantly more with less as both knowledge and know-how increase; to "synergetics," the behavior of whole systems unobserved in their parts; and to a "world game" played on computers in lieu of the vain and murderous politics of men. The great appeal of Fuller's utopian vision, naïve as it may be about human perversity, rests on his belief that "universe is not a failure."

There are, of course, still many other cross-currents in the Sixties, more significant in a cultural or ideological sense than in any academic definition of intellectual discipline. The Black Power movement takes *The Autobiography of Malcolm X* (1965) and Frantz Fanon's *The Wretched of the Earth* (1968) as its central statements. Women's Lib draws on Betty Friedan's *The Feminine Mystique* (1963), Kate Millett's *Sexual Politics* (1970), and Germaine Greer's *The Female Eunuch* (1970). The ecological movement, which goes back to Rachel Carson's *Silent Spring* (1962), finds more dire predictions in Paul Ehrlich's *The Population Bomb*

(1968) and Barry Commoner's *The Closing Circle* (1972). The "death of God" theologians refer to Thomas J. J. Altizer's and William Hamilton's *Radical Theology and the Death of God* (1966). Timothy Leary's *The Politics of Ecstacy* (1968) offers a dubious manifesto of psychedelics on the wane. The new eroticism, camp or pornographic, profits from the relaxation of censorship since Grove Press defends its right to publish D. H. Lawrence's *Lady Chatterly's Lover* and Henry Miller's *Tropic of Cancer* in 1960–62. At the same time, sophisticated knowledge of sexual behavior, derived from scientific experiments recorded in William H. Masters's and Virginia E. Johnson's *Human Sexual Response* (1966), becomes widely available. Encounter groups, gestalt therapy, and sensitivity training also become fashionable. And ethology, deriving from Konrad Lorenz's animal studies and Robert Ardrey's popularization of African anthropology, advances a different view of man's aggressive nature, exemplified in Lionel Tiger's and Robin Fox's *The Imperial Animal* (1971). Finally, education returns to a progressive and student-centered vision, first propounded by John Dewey in the Thirties, in such works as Carl R. Rogers's *Freedom to Learn* (1969) and George B. Leonard's *Education and Ecstacy* (1968). Which of these many trends may gain or lose momentum in the Seventies, at this time only seers may know.

Among all the intellectual genres of the postwar period, one gradually proves more congenial to the literary temper than many others. The genre cuts across traditional disciplines and recovers the old free form of the essay. Indeed, the new journalistic essay often compounds prose and poetry, biography and analysis, anecdote and polemic. Thus it attempts to acknowledge the stresses of culture, the pressures of the Self, the tensions of the imagination. Thus, too, it permits both author and reader to create a place for their *person* amid the complexities of the world. Significantly, some of the most compelling examples of this "higher journalism" come out of Black experience. Hence the forceful line of sensibility that runs through James Baldwin's *Notes of a Native Son* (1955), *Nobody Knows My Name* (1961), and *The Fire Next Time* (1963); *The Autobiography of Malcolm X* (1965); and Eldridge Cleaver's *Soul on Ice* (1968). In a much more modish vein, Tom Wolfe's *The Kandy-Kolored Tangerine-Flake Streamlined Baby* (1965), *The Pump House Gang* (1968), and *The Electric Kool-Aid Acid Test* (1968) dramatize various aspects of manners and morals in America.

But the most original practitioners of the new essay may be John Cage and Norman Mailer. Cage, an apostle of avant-garde movements in music, dance, theatre, art, also turns his extraordinary attention to social, to human, problems in *Silence* (1961) and *A Year from Monday* (1967). Experimenting with typography and computerized random operations based mainly on the *I Ching*, he is able to draw on ideas of Suzuki, Duchamp, Brown, Fuller, and McLuhan, on innumerable other sources and anecdotes of his own, to formulate a discontinuous statement both practical and visionary, acknowledging technology in the spirit of Zen.

Mailer, on the other hand, approaches the great questions of the moment magically, and acknowledges them in the spirit of the heroic ego. His *Armies of the Night* (1968), *Miami and the Siege of Chicago* (1968), *Of a Fire on the Moon* (1970), and *The Prisoner of Sex* (1971), create an uncanny persona of the author, at once self-critical and over-assertive, strong, quick, and cunning enough to expose the paranoia of the times. The persona improvises itself on the breath of a style unique in American letters.

Although literary critics seldom compare with such men as Mailer, Cage, Brown, Fuller, McLuhan, and Marcuse in arousing the passions of readers or in commanding an original perception of the times, they enjoy a certain prestige, a degree of visibility. Their essays invade academic journals as well as little magazines, sometimes edging poetry and fiction out of sight. Their books exhibit resourceful diversity in both theory and practice, and help to create the climate of literary opinion. Hence the rubric an "age of criticism," which some writers apply to the Forties and early Fifties.

During the early postwar years, the influence of the New Criticism predominates. Conceived in the Thirties by a group of gifted Southern writers, many of whom are poets and novelists as well as critics, the New Criticism is formalist in its aesthetics, agrarian in political economy, and Christian in religious outlook. This is clear in the manifesto *I'll Take My Stand: The South and the Agrarian Tradition* (1930), to which John Crowe Ransom, Allen Tate, Cleanth Brooks, Robert Penn Warren, and Donald Davidson contribute; and clear again in Ransom's own work, *The New Criticism* (1941), which gives the movement its name. The revolt of the New Critics against the drab historicism of much current literary scholarship, their insistence on the organic wholeness of the literary work, their virtuosity in explicating texts and eliciting the complex meanings of words, their sensitivity to the nuances of irony, allusion, and metaphor—all these inspire widespread emulation. Thus the New Criticism becomes the new critical orthodoxy in various universities across the nation, extending its influence through such quarterlies as the *Kenyon Review* and the *Sewanee Review*, and through such popular textbooks of formalism as Cleanth Brooks and Robert Penn Warren's *Understanding Poetry* (1938, 1950, 1960) and *Understanding Fiction* (1943, 1950, 1959).

But the formalist movement, which stresses the autonomous and formal character of all art, is wider in scope than the New Criticism itself; nor are all adherents of that movement

natives of the American South. Among the most gifted formalists, R. P. Blackmur, a New Englander, proves his versatility in critical essays, intuitive and darkly flashing, collected
in *Language and Gesture* (1952) and *The Lion and the
Honeycomb* (1954). René Wellek combines his special interest in Russian and Czech formalism with the breadth of
his European scholarship in a classic text, co-authored with
Austin Warren, *Theory of Literature* (1949). Susanne Langer
draws on Kantian philosophy as well as on semantics and
anthropology to formulate her aesthetic in *Form and Feeling*
(1953). The Chicago school of neo-Aristotelian formalists,
comprising R. S. Crane, Elder Olson, W. R. Keast, and Richard McKeon, signal their achievement in a large anthology
that Crane edits, *Critics and Criticism, Ancient and Modern*
(1952). And the Canadian scholar Northrop Frye offers in
The Anatomy of Criticism (1957) a brilliant theoretical study
based on exhaustive knowledge of literature, myth, ritual, and
archetype. The study evolves an original literary typology
that forces formalism beyond textual analysis.

Except Frye, all these critics belong to an older generation;
they begin to publish before the war. Their authority, nevertheless, sanctions a vast exegetical enterprise well into the
Fifties. Yet even before that time, some younger critics note
that formalism may have extended and refined itself too
far. They turn to other approaches: psychoanalytic, mythographic, sociological. They seek, particularly, a criticism attentive to the literary qualities of the text, yet vivid in its
cultural perceptions.

In this restoration of criticism to a larger view, Lionel
Trilling plays a special part. Standing between the old and
new generation of critics, Trilling begins to publish his remarkable essays in the Thirties, though his books appear only
after the war. These books include three distinguished titles:
The Liberal Imagination (1950), *The Opposing Self* (1955),
and *Beyond Culture* (1965). Without consciously assuming

the leadership of any critical school, Trilling provides an alternative to formalist doctrines and, at the same time, a corrective to liberal and radical ideologies, the very same ideologies against which formalism itself stands. Trilling's subtle and profound grasp of both the literary and social facts of the last two hundred years, his intellectual poise between the great ideas of the Enlightenment and the great passions of Romanticism, his intuitions into the cultural region wherein, say, Matthew Arnold and Sigmund Freud may meet to define the crisis of the modern mind—all these remain exemplary. But his aloofness toward postwar literature and his rather too cautionary attitude toward the "subversive" element in modern art—the element of spirit or Self unmediated by the rationalities of history—qualify the impact of his ideas on younger critics. Trilling's novel, *The Middle of the Journey* (1947), captures the central ambivalences of the times and of his own temperament.

Alfred Kazin, also a critic of broad cultural concerns, writes his best book, *On Native Grounds* (1942), about the period between 1890 and 1940 in American letters. Though Kazin has genuine moral intensity in his finest criticism, his subsequent works, *The Inmost Leaf* (1955) and *Contemporaries* (1962), show an uncertain response to current trends. Increasingly, he assumes the easy role of the civilized reviewer rather than the literary thinker. His autobiographical work, *A Walker in the City* (1951), renders his colorful and moving sense of New York life in an earlier age.

Taking more risks than either Trillling or Kazin, Leslie Fiedler also shows himself to be more attuned to the contemporary element. He begins his career with an obsessive interest in certain categories of myth and archetype. These categories he employs, in the essays of *An End to Innocence* (1955), to clarify racial, sexual, political, geographical, and literary aspects of America. The archetypal figures of the Jew, the Indian, the Negro, among others, serve Fiedler as focus of artistic and historical energies of the country. In his major work, *Love and Death in the American Novel* (1960, 1966), Fiedler goes farther in exploring the underside of formative myths, the patterns that shape both social character and literary fiction, that shape particularly the traditions of the gothic, picaresque, and sentimental novels from Charles Brockden Brown to Herman Wouk. *No! In Thunder* (1960), *Waiting for the End* (1964), and *The Return of the Vanishing American* (1968) combine Fiedler's active interests in popular culture and the literary avant-garde. At times erratic, more often provocative and inventive as a critic, Fiedler also writes fiction—*Pull Down Vanity* (1962), *The Second Stone* (1963), *Back to China* (1965), *The Last Jew in America* (1966), *Nude Croquet* (1969)—and an autobiographical work, *Being Busted* (1969).

Besides Fiedler, the critics who address themselves specifically to postwar society and literature remain few. John W. Aldridge is perhaps the first to recognize the new fiction in *After the Lost Generation* (1951). His other critical works, *In Search of Heresy* (1956), *Time to Murder and Create* (1966), and *The Devil in the Fire* (1972), expand his initial concern with literary manners. Eloquent—his critiques of Mailer are among the best of that complex figure—and sometimes intolerant, Aldridge writes his most controversial work, *In the Country of the Young* (1970), about the cultural significance of the youth movement of the Sixties.

Witty and curious, Benjamin DeMott collects his essays in *Hells and Benefits* (1962), *You Don't Say* (1966), and *Supergrow* (1969). His ironic intelligence ranges, at times superficially, over countless topics: mass media, homosexuality, the United States Senate, faculty clubs, sex research, the teaching of English, rock music, student radicals, racial hatred in Mississippi, Hollywood fantasies, Vietnam. Although DeMott's voice can be tiresomely hip and flip, his commitment to the enhancement of the imagination in American life is abiding.

A former editor of *Partisan Review*, Richard Poirier approaches current issues with a show of ardor. His earlier studies, *The Comic Sense of Henry James* (1960) and *A World Elsewhere* (1966), offer fine stylistic analyses of American literature. But Poirier's interest in contemporary culture declares itself only in *The Performing Self* (1971). In that work, Poirier seeks to define models of "performance," both literary and political, and thus to distinguish the recent achievements of Borges and Nabokov, Mailer and Barth, the Beatles and the Rolling Stones, from the traditional assumptions of humanism. Examples of cultural violence, such as the "war on the young," and instances of "self-parody," "de-creation," and "waste," from Joyce to Pynchon, amplify his theme.

Susan Sontag is another writer inward with contemporary trends. Although her brilliant observations in *Against Interpretation* (1966) and *Styles of Radical Will* (1969) grate on less venturesome critics, her analyses of such phenomena as camp, happenings, pornography, science fiction, and "the new sensibility," are often both accurate and original. Sontag also writes with flair about film, theatre, and politics, and in recent years directs some films herself. Her insights into art and society falter when, insisting too much on her hard-edged intelligence, she evades the emotional or spiritual nuances of her subject. To some extent, this failure affects her two teasing novels, *The Benefactor* (1963) and *Death Kit* (1967).

The main pursuit of Ihab Hassan is also avant-garde literature, the emergence of the new. His first work, *Radical Innocence* (1961) is a critique of postwar fiction, centering on the concept of the anti-hero as a rebel-victim. In *The Literature of Silence* (1967), Hassan begins to examine a developing theme: the need of art first to doubt, then to subvert or transcend, its own forms and authority. The critical theme of "silence" appears in fuller perspective in Hassan's next work, *The Dismemberment of Orpheus* (1971). But in his latest essays, which he calls Paracriticism, Hassan experiments with a discontinuous medium, mixing literary and non-literary materials, mixing expository and other modes of discourse, questioning the critical act itself even as he hopes to redefine it.

What distinguishes all these critics from earlier formalists is their active concern with cultural issues and with current literature. They are not alone, of course, in such concerns. Isaac Rosenfeld in *An Age of Enormity* (1962), Robert Warshow in *The Immediate Experience* (1962), Irving Howe in *A World More Attractive* (1963), Norman Podhoretz in *Doings and Undoings* (1964) and *Making It* (1968), and Richard Kostelanetz in many works, notably *Master Minds* (1969), contribute to the cultural sense of the period. So do novelists contribute in such works of non-fiction as Wright Morris's *A Bill of Rights, A Bill of Wrongs, A Bill of Goods* (1968), and Gore Vidal's *Reflections on a Sinking Ship* (1969).

The reaction against formalism, however, takes another direction among academic critics who are preoccupied with theoretical questions and with the literature of the past. Murray Krieger accurately discerns that direction as a flight from the discrete analysis of texts, from the pretense of distance and objectivity in literary interpretation. In such books as *The Tragic Vision* (1960) and *A Window to Criticism* (1964), Krieger himself moves part of the way in that direction, without denying the concrete reality, the mediating power, of the work of art, and without denying the necessity of criticism.

By contrast, Harold Bloom wants to overcome the sullen discreteness of the single text. A critic learned in the mythic and mystic traditions of poetry, entranced by the primal effort of the creative imagination, Bloom sees all great works of literature as acts of continuous participation in an organic, an encompassing, vision of love. Quite fittingly, his books, which include *The Visionary Company* (1961, 1971), *Blake's Apocalypse* (1963), and *The Ringers in the Tower* (1971), aspire to reshape our understanding of all Romantic poetry.

The presence of certain European modes of thought may be felt in the approach of Bloom, and even more in the work of J. Hillis Miller, Geoffrey Hartman, and Paul de Man. These modes of thought include structuralism (Claude Lévi-Strauss), phenomenology (Edmund Husserl, Martin Heidegger, Maurice Merleau-Ponty, Gaston Bachelard), linguistics (Ferdinand de Saussure, Roman Jakobson), psycholinguistics (Jacques Lacan), semiotics and grammatology (Roland Barthes, Jacques Derrida), the Geneva criticism of consciousness (Georges Poulet, Jean-Pierre Richard, Jean Starobinski), hermeneutics (Wilhelm Dilthey, Hans Georg Gadamer), the archaeology of knowledge (Michel Foucault), and perhaps the criticism of negativity (Maurice Blanchot). Within the context of these European influences, which are sometimes loosely labeled as structuralist, Miller's *Poets of Reality* (1965), Hartman's *Beyond Formalism* (1970), and de Man's *Blindness and Insight* (1971) delimit an important area of critical attention and theoretical inquiry in America. Thus, a new field of literary consciousness comes to supplant the New Criticism of another age.

But what of the changes in postwar literature itself? These seem more elusive than the changes in non-fiction or criticism. Still, the years throw a certain pattern in relief. In the Forties, writers gradually break away from naturalism as they begin to evolve new attitudes toward their war-torn experiences. With the blessings of the New Critics, they favor mythic, elegant, or complex forms. By the mid Fifties, the structures of literature begin to open themselves to a more jagged, roguish, or grotesque sense of reality; and the novel, leading the way, reinvents the gothic and picaresque modes. The lines that separate comedy from tragedy, pathos from irony, that distinguish rigid from improvisational forms, tend to blur. In the Sixties, literature shows increased tolerance for chance and incongruity. Eroticism, fantasy, gallows humor, comic surrealism, the absurdist manner prevail. Some authors carry these tendencies into the Seventies toward a "literature of silence" that mocks its own origins.

Looking back on the postwar period as a whole, we can also distinguish a few movements and breakthroughs that are likely to become part of literary history. We can recognize that the works of certain minorities and subcultures attain a high order of excellence, acquire a special kind of urgency. Thus, Jewish authors command unprecedented attention by the brilliance of their imagination, by their sheer numbers. The Beat Movement, short in span and ambiguous in achievement, still injects a new energy into the period. Drawing on European existentialism, on Oriental mysticism, on American strains of rhapsodic dissent and transcendental affirmation—Thoreau, Emerson, Whitman—the movement speaks of natural and spontaneous man in open or improvised forms. Black literature also grows in diversity, in intensity, with the growth of the Black Power movement. More conscious of its ethnic heritage and political trials than ever before, this literature draws on the anger, dignity, and hope of new Black writers. Finally, cutting across genres and subcultures, a fantastic vision, grim but also antic, challenging the assumptions of any culture, of being itself, looks toward the future. At ease in the void and erudite in absurdity, this postexistential vision still finds its inspiration in something other than contemporary nihilism: it wants to re-form human consciousness even at the expense of its own art. A gnostic desire to apprehend the human condition under the aspect of pure spirit trembles into language.

II

FICTION

INTRODUCTION

When Hemingway and Faulkner die, in 1961 and 1962 respectively, the new fiction is already fully fledged. Many major novelists of the Twenties and Thirties continue, of course, to publish after World War II; but hints of a different social and aesthetic climate are seen in a number of authors who first make themselves known in the Forties. These authors, important as they may be, can be treated here only in a transitional manner; they serve as precursors of postwar fiction.

Of these, perhaps the most influential, certainly the most elusive, is Vladimir Nabokov (born 1899). He defies the schemes of literary history. Born in Russia, he emigrates to Germany, next to France, then to America in 1940, returning to Europe in 1960 to live in Switzerland. He writes novels in Russian, in French, and in English, the language that grants him fame. Though considerably older than postwar novelists, he leads the way, word and chess player, a fantasist of the absolute. Though he is naturalized only in 1945, he creates in *Lolita* (1955, 1958) a monstrously true and merry statement about life in America. His novels written originally in English include *The Real Life of Sebastian Knight* (1941), *Bend Sinister* (1947), *Lolita, Pnin* (1957), *Pale Fire* (1962), perhaps his best, and *Ada* (1969), perhaps his most ambitious. They reveal a self-delighting mind, recovering through shifting parodic patterns of language some lost vista of memory, some love or artifice of eternity. Throughout his work the theme of man's life in dream or art plays around the edge of reality until the reality burns in insubstantial fire. Still, the cerebral quality of Nabokov prevails even in his explorations of bizarre sensuality; his prodigious wit and learning, his characters and plots, can become too rare or wan. Young writers who admire him most tend to be experimentalists, absurdists of the novel, or simply cool talents who find in the antic impatience of the master a reflection of nihilism.

By contrast, James Gould Cozzens (born 1903) seems uneasy in his relation to the postwar world. His best work, *Guard of Honor* (1948), deals with Negro segregation in a Southern Air Force base. An innate conservative, he stresses the limitations of men, the enduring stability of institutions. First ignored, then sporadically prized, his works, from *The Last Adam* (1933) to *By Love Possessed* (1957), are often turgid novels of manners, traditional in their form as in their concerns, yet not entirely devoid of moral power. Cozzens, who is descended from Colonial Tories, represents an old-fashioned sense of the American experience—it may be identified with the "WASP" class—a sense that rarely inspires contemporary fiction. Its attractions lie precisely in its certitudes among dissolving values, a kind of stoic nostalgia.

Conservative in a different way, Robert Penn Warren (born 1905) is a writer of greater skill and force. His original associations are with the brilliant Southern movement which, in the Thirties, included the New Critics and the Fugitive Poets. Skeptical of reason, science, and industrialism, of romantic individualism and the frontier legend as well, Warren seeks in religious myth and Christian metaphor a definition of the human community, of fulfilled identity. His distinguished novel *All the King's Men* (1946), suggested by the career of Huey Long, the great Louisiana demagogue, forces politics into the frame of more complex and enduring truths. In subsequent novels—*World Enough and Time* (1950), *Band of Angels* (1955), and *The Cave* (1960), for instance —Warren sometimes repeats himself in overwrought manner; yet his imagination holds character and history in tension, and his drive toward a dramatic knowledge of redemption gives dignity to the novelist's enterprise.

Warren reflects the transition from naturalism to symbolism which so many postwar novelists assume as complete. Nelson Algren (born 1909), more sentimental about the colorful and seamy sides of cities, modifies naturalism with poetry and wild humor. His best novel, *The Man With the Golden Arm* (1949), is a taut, frightening tale of dope addiction in Chicago, moved by great compassion. But in Algren's later work, *A Walk on the Wild Side* (1956) or *The Neon Wilderness* (1958), anger shows a soft lurid edge. A radical eccentric, ebullient even in pessimism, his perceptions have a certain extravagance that prefigures both the black humor and existential rebelliousness of later decades.

But the directions of the new fiction are far more various than Cozzens, Warren, and Algren can suggest. In broad terms, its development seems a continuous movement from realism toward a new surrealism, toward a loosening of forms, toward silence and self-parody, toward the inspired absurdities of John Barth's *Lost in the Fun House* (1968). Moving in time, the postwar novel also recognizes the enormous diversity of American culture viewed at any given moment as a spatial artifact. Between the appearances of that culture—clichés of mass media or technocratic bureaucracy—and its inner motives, between the normative images of the first and the opposing images of the last, a huge discrepancy obtains. The opposing Self pursues beyond disaffiliation a new concept of love or of freedom. The pursuit of love brings men to the threshold of mystical experience and the search for freedom brings them to the frontiers of nihilism; thus, saintliness and crime violently merge in quest of a new consciousness.

The hero, vicar of the Self in the new fiction, serves to mediate the contradictions of culture. His dominant aspect is that of the rebel-victim. He is an actor but also a sufferer. Almost always, he is an outsider, a demonic or sacrificial figure, anarchic, grotesque, innocent or clownish, wavering still between martyrdom and frenzied self-affirmation. Thus, the rebel-victim incarnates the eternal dialectic of the primary Yes and the everlasting No; and his function is to create those values whose absence in culture is the cause of his predicament and ours. His morality is largely existential, defined by his actions and even more by his passions, a self-made morality, full of ironies and ambiguities. The will of the hero, however, is always in some sense redemptive; he differs from the mythic scapegoat only in his allegiance to the forms of art.

Like the ancient hero with a thousand faces, it is natural that the rebel-victim should assume many guises. Here, for instance, are ten of his disguises: (1) the child who stands for truth or innocence, violated by existence; (2) the lonely and quixotic adolescent, never confirmed in his initiation, exposing the corruptions of the adult world; (3) the young lover, caught in the oppositions of instinct and society, in those of his own dreams; (4) the comic rogue, traveling through a crowded life with verve, but sadly finding for himself no home or mate; (5) the grotesque, insisting upon his particular vision of things, twisting reality to conform to the distortions of his own spirit; (6) the stubborn underdog, the poor and underprivileged, defying still the oppressions of some system; (7) the disinherited American, expatriate, finding no end to alienation; (8) the Black, Indian, Jew, or Hipster, outsider within his own country, trying to create for himself, beyond hatred or guilt, an identity; (9) the sexual deviant, condemned to a life of violence or ostracism; (10) the jolly nihilist, cosmic and futile jester, vaudevillian of the dark, calling all of life into question.

As the fictional hero attempts to mediate the contradictions of culture, and even to create a new consciousness, so does the form of the novel itself attempt the same task on a deeper level. Realism and surrealism, comedy and tragedy, event and symbol tend to fuse in evasive forms, equal to the perplexities of the day. Between the irrational force of human instincts and the insane power of the superstate, the novel strikes its own incongruous bargains with terror and slapstick, poetry and fantasy. The fiction of Joyce, Kafka, or Beckett displays greater technical virtuosity. But the American postwar novel, with its special knowledge of violence, becomes a "connoisseur of chaos." Its language mimes its way madly, merrily, to desperate truth. Thus, the novel meets the challenge that one of its practitioners, Philip Roth, defines in an essay, "Writing American Fiction" (1961):

> And what is the moral of so long a story? Simply this: that the American writer in the middle of the 20th century has his hands full in trying to understand, and then describe, and then make *credible* much of the American reality. It stupefies, it sickens, it infuriates, and finally it is even a kind of embarrassment to one's own meager imagination.

MAJOR NOVELISTS

Saul Bellow

Saul Bellow (born 1915) is among the first of postwar writers to declare the promise of the new literature. Born in Canada, he grows up in Chicago during the Thirties, sweeping past the entrenched naturalism of that era. Like all writers of magnitude, he puts his stamp on reality in a style recognizably his own. He brings a strong sense of the traditional European novel—Balzac, Dickens, Dostoevski—to his freewheeling American art. An intellectual read widely in philosophy and history, sociology and anthropology, a novelist of ideas foremost, he still chooses the turbulence of city streets as the ambiance of his fiction. His urban Jewish characters, conscious of their ancient heritage, embody the perplexities of the American Jew seeking a new consciousness of himself, a new definition of his fate. Similarly, Bellow's language recovers elements of the Yiddish oral tradition for literary use. But the central quest of his work is persistently larger: he asks how man may survive as a creature fully possessed of his humanity, in touch with the "axial lines of existence," in a tangled world. The quest is typically comic; the seeking hero, suffering, laughing, always physically or spiritually on the move, often assumes the role of the neo-picaresque. Bellow's humor, however ribald or anguished the occasion seems, humanizes failure; and even his grotesques show some honor. As one of his minor characters, old Schlossberg, puts it: "Have dignity, you understand me? Choose dignity. Nobody knows enough to turn it down." Bellow's narrative, usually in the confessional mode of autobiography, journal, or letter, makes a place for conscience in the midst of flux. He explores as well the archetypal American themes,

sex and success, power and death, in contexts that demand
a new vision. But as the times change ever more rapidly,
Bellow seems to retrench. In his most recent work, he draws
back from the extremes of contemporary experience, betrays
a certain querulousness. The inestimable gift of awareness,
which he lavishes upon his best characters, becomes a little
scantier; and his forms display less inventiveness.

Bellow's first novel, *Dangling Man* (1944), owes more to
the example of Kafka or Dostoevski than of Dreiser. Its hero,
Joseph, reveals the ironies of existential man, caught between
metaphysical absurdity and social regimentation in wartime
America. With the acrid naïveté that is the basis of his character, Joseph faces all the possibilities of *freedom*, freedom
to act and to understand, only to retreat into the army at
the crucial moment. Alienation, he senses, is a "fools' plea,"
for the world lies within us. Yet in the end he is forced to
confess: "I had not done well alone." Turned inward upon
itself, colorless in style and thinly dramatic, the novel establishes a certain mood of postwar fiction—grim fantasy and
scratchy intelligence—rather than a measure of its author's
ability.

The Victim (1947), carries the mummery of guilt, dread,
and self-justification farther. Addressing itself explicitly to
anti-Semitism in America, the novel spins around two characters, Kirby Allbee and Asa Levanthal, one Gentile and the
other Jew, really a Double, creating a universal fable of
human ambiguities. Who is his brother's keeper and why?
Reversal follows reversal. It is Allbee, for instance, who
poses as the aggrieved party and cries: "'Know thyself'!
Everybody knows but nobody wants to admit." The final
irony is in that identification of antagonists which Leventhal
experiences as he looks at the back of Allbee's neck, feeling
his presence as his own. Dour, ironic, and compassionate, the
book finds a form adequate to its human complexities.
Notably, it stands as a landmark of serious Jewish fiction,

taking bold measure of its cultural moment, correlating the theme of racial prejudice to the pursuit of status and money, to the deathly motives of a vast competitive order.

But the turning point in Bellow's career comes with *The Adventures of Augie March* (1953), which jolts the author into fame. Moving toward a more open form, making richer use of the variousness of his Chicago experiences, Bellow shapes all into a language of the Self seeking a "special fate." Augie's character is his fate, balanced within the concentric circles of his Jewish family, his big city, and the midcentury culture of his raucous country. Humorous and headlong, the narrative carries Augie through many episodes, erotic encounters, shady dealings of men, the ins and outs and dead ends of the American Dream. Yet innocent in some ways to the end, perhaps a trifle the *schlemiel,* he can still say: "I did have opposition in me, and great desire to offer resistance and to say 'No!'" Evading corruption, "world-wide Babylonishness," avoiding despair, Augie hears in laughter the mystery of life: "That's the *animal ridens* in me, the laughing creatures forever rising up." This big book restores wonder and a certain blatancy to fiction and sets an example to writers who have surrendered their art to Jamesian refinements or Jungian myths. But the book is not entirely blameless either in its verbal conceits or in its occasional lapses between what Augie, the narrator, *can* see and Bellow, the author, *must* render.

At the height of his creative powers, Bellow returns to the leaner form of the novella and writes, in *Seize the Day* (1956), a brief masterpiece on the human encounter with error, with death itself. Moneyless and all too mortal, Tommy Wilhelm finally gains an inner perspective in which failure ceases to be a personal thing and death no longer seems the final degradation, the apotheosis of all errors. Against the pretender-soul, full of the world's cunning and vanity, he

✓ affirms the true-soul, akin to love, released in vast and self-less sorrow.

But of all Bellow's works, it is *Henderson the Rain King* (1958) that leaves the most expansive sense of life. Frankly conceived as a romance, a quest through Africa visited by Bellow only in the mind the novel raises fantasy, desire, and perception to the level of wisdom. Henderson's heart cries: "I want, I want, I want." Yet he commits himself to an ideal of service or altruism—of Sir Wilfred Grenfell, of Albert Schweitzer—that he understands at last in the presence of a sacred lioness. Henderson is huge, passionate, rich, and middle-aged, driven toward a life of heroic failures and clownish quests. He says: "The physical is all there, and it belongs to science. But then there is the noumenal department, and there we create and create and create." Believing that the "forgiveness of sins is perpetual and righteousness first is not required," he throws himself into life, "some powerful magnificence not human." But he also knows death too well, the cosmic coldness in the eyes of an octopus. His final intuition of Being, achieved among high African adventures that reflect back upon Western civilization, is sustained by a magic style, leaping here and there with waggish or woeful exuberance. Thus, the endless availability of Augie gives way to the greater mystery of Henderson's responsibility, to the vitality of altruistic desire.

Bellow has not to date surpassed the achievement of that work. *Herzog* (1964), a quasi-epistolary novel, though it bristles with metaphor and idea, ends by giving a confined sense of fate. Lucid at times, biting with the double edge of self-pity, Herzog, despite all his letters, does not carry the reader to a perception larger than his own. His intelligence remains haunted by some of the very fears it claims to exorcise.

In *Mr. Sammler's Planet* (1970) Bellow disciplines himself into a firmer moral tone. Placing man between past and future, history and science fiction—there are many references to H. G. Wells in the book—old Mr. Sammler copes with the present only in terms of his humanist loyalties. A survivor of Nazi mass murders and burials, Sammler has also known literary Bloomsbury and now makes his home among the terrors of New York. (His encounter with a Black is one of the most charged scenes of the novel.) But Sammler's durable memory and "civil heart" are finally inadequate to the monstrosities of the modern world. There is a narrowness, a primness of vision, which inhibits his capacity to love or prophesy.

The energy of Bellow's imagination, once dominant in contemporary literature, seems to wait upon deeper fulfillment. As he himself writes in one of his rare essays: "We have so completely debunked the old idea of the Self that we can hardly continue in the same way. . . . Undeniably the human being is not what he commonly thought a century ago. The question nevertheless remains. He is something. What is he?" It is doubtful that Bellow has given us, in his later fiction, the most compelling answer to the enigma of man.

Norman Mailer

Perhaps more than any other American writer, Norman Mailer (born 1925) appears as the chief representative of the age. This claim rests on the extraordinary vitality of his imagination, his readiness to respond to the largest problems of the times in original manner—rests, indeed, on his power to shape the moment rather than on any specific masterpiece of fiction. Like Hemingway, he creates a brawling legend of his life, and the legend comes to be a projection of his energy as much as any work of art. At the center of both life and art, a great ambition persists: to wrest from the contradictions of history and nature, from the warring cosmos itself, a finer fate for man. This romantic heroism of Mailer's, this cult of courage, is qualified on the one hand by intellectual wit and qualified on the other by a mystic and erotic intuition of existence; modern ideas and primitive magic keep his spirit on the stretch. Manichaean in his metaphysics, he sees the world as the product of an unfinished struggle between God and the Devil, a struggle to which man daily contributes. Thus, in a divided universe, the *quality* of power tips continuously the scales of Life and Death.

At every turn, Mailer resists the technocratic or totalitarian organization of the human psyche, which he identifies with cancer, excrement, entropy, with death moving into contemporary society. Forever, he seeks the life spark in the smells of love, in a dangerous gesture, in the thrust of the imagination. His own intellectual development provides a critique of changing American values. Liberalism, Marxism, Hipsterism, the New Left serve as successive stages in an ideological revaluation of the possibilities of life, a radical review of history. Similarly, Mailer's art undergoes mutations of its own. Breaking with realism early, his novels adapt symbolic and pop forms. The style becomes increasingly more supple, colorful, humorous, distinctive. Later still, Mailer explores a new form of the times, hybrid of history and fiction, confession and controversy.

One of the best and best-selling war novels still, *The Naked and the Dead* (1948) presents an overview of soldiers on an island in the Pacific. The image of the army, "like a nest of ants wrestling and tugging at a handful of bread crumbs in a field of grass," conveys the randomness and force of instincts at work. But the blundering campaign of Anopopei also mirrors vaster political issues pertaining to the postwar world. The various symbolic levels of the novel are dramatized in the conflict between three central characters: General Cummings, a visionary totalitarian; Lieutenant Hearn, a misanthropic liberal; and Sergeant Croft, a demonic individualist. Horror, defeat, and death prevail; the drive toward omnipotence, as private motive or historical destiny, fails. It is a world without regenerative powers, projecting its decay into the future, presaging a crisis of which the war is only a part. Still, the impact of the novel derives from its vision— fractured by Mailer's narrative shifts, "Chorus" sections, and "Time Machine" flashbacks—of dispossessed humanity from "the raucous stricken bosom of America," waiting for some emergent fate. Thus, Mailer takes his first long step beyond the pieties of ordinary war fiction, and becomes instantly famous.

His fame recedes for nearly a decade. When his next two novels appear, many critics call them unmitigated disasters —now as many find in them great redeeming traits. In both works, Mailer strains for a new conception of his art, even of himself. In *Barbary Shore* (1951), he writes a febrile allegory concerning the failure of revolutionary politics, reflected in the lives of various seedy characters sharing a Brooklyn rooming house. The characters form fragments of a puzzle: Hollingsworth, the capitalist with fascist leanings; McLeod the Marxist with Bolshevist affiliations; Lovett, the Trotskyite narrator suffering from amnesia. In addition, a deranged, innocent girl, Lonnie, used sexually by everyone, and an aging Hollywood drop-out, Guinevere, remind us that the puzzle may be more psychological than ideological. Melodramatic in parts, surrealistic in others, the novel reaches for a new perception of politics and eroticism united in madness.

With *The Deer Park* (1955), Mailer becomes more explicitly the hierophant of sexual mysteries; and his political passion begins to take existential hues. Set in a luxurious desert colony of Hollywood stars and film makers, the book exposes with equivocal comedy the nihilism, cowardice, and hypocrisy of a symbolic segment of American society. Like the orgiastic playground of Louis XV, from which the novel

derives its title, Desert D'Or is really built of dreams, the
pleasures of self-deception. We are in a mirrored hall of Hell.
Only the pimp Marion Faye, ruthless and unillusioned, can
subsist in that demesne. The narrator, Sergius O'Shaugnessy,
escapes because he remains open to love and danger. The
novel, however, remains willed, strenuous in its shifts of
point of view, vibrant only in certain scenes.

It is in a collection of essays and stories, *Advertisements
for Myself* (1959), that Mailer finds his true voice, the right
timbre and style of an apocalyptic imagination, the release
of his ambition. "The sour truth is that I am imprisoned with
a perception which will settle for nothing less than making
a revolution in the consciousness of our time," he states in
the first advertisement. Admonishing himself, he admonishes
also the age: "I still feel rage at the cowardice of our time
which has ground down all of us into the mediocre com-
promises of what had been once our light-filled passion to
stand erect and be original." The crucial essay, "The White
Negro," defines the mystique of the Hipster: American exis-
tentialist, obeying the "rebellious imperatives of the self,"
attuned to danger and the music of his instincts. In a sense,
the White Negro turns the collective death of the age against
itself; with murder and creation in his heart, he strives to
keep man alive. The other pieces in the book confirm the
image of Mailer as prophet and outrageous clown, an inspired
intelligence—sometimes nasty or erratic—taking on the whole
of culture in quest of a new vision. *The Presidential Papers*
(1963) and *Cannibals and Christians* (1966) continue that
tradition of shamanistic commentary.

But Mailer also pursues his experiments with the novel in
two highly successful works written in his new-found style:
An American Dream (1965) and *Why Are We in Vietnam?*
(1967). In the first, Mailer impersonates the writer of hard-
boiled, action-packed, lurid detective stories, to create an
American myth deeper than parody, taller than the tall tale.

Humor and obscenity abound, and even self-derision, yet none of these vitiates the heroic drive toward action and knowledge, "the ability to hold the maximum of impossible combinations in one's mind." The hero, Stephen Rojack, intellectual athlete, Kennedy *manqué*, enters into a moon-struck compact with love and death, experiences all the evils that a metropolis like New York can offer in thirty-two violent hours, including the magic struggle between White and Black, and emerges on the other side of loss and terror, still affirming the ambiguous possibilities of life in America. He loses his beloved, Cherry, to the dark, yet he also saves his courage, his sanity, and a kind of innocence of the flesh: "In some, madness must come in with breath, mill through the blood and be breathed out again. In some it goes up to the mind. . . . Cancer is the growth of madness denied." Intense, sensual and droll, the style reveals through its uncanny texture, its animism, its smell, a mysterious realm where gods and demons still grapple for the liberty of man.

In *Why Are We in Vietnam?* Mailer impersonates the voice of a youthful White Texan, D. J., "America's own wandering troubadour," who may also be a "black-ass cripple Spade" from Harlem. The scabrous story treats the Vietnam war obliquely; it relates a climactic hunt for grizzly bear in the Brooks Range of Alaska, within the Arctic Circle, where all the invisible forces of the nation converge. The hunt, reminiscent of Faulkner's *The Bear*, initiates D. J. into the deep corruptions of his elders, the primal force of instinct, and the murderous love of comrades. Despite the sly ambiguities in point of view, the narrative and dramatic structures of the novel stand firm. Thus the various conflicts between D. J.'s father, Rusty, and his mother, Hallie; between father and son; between the hunting party and their professional guide, Big Luke; between D. J. and his best friend, Tex; between men and beasts—all these re-create a myth of "that sad deep sweet beauteous mystery land of purple forests, and pink rock, and blue water . . . , " charged with the "undiscovered magnetic-electro fief of the dream." The insanity of American violence appears as a perversion of the very conditions of freedom and vitality in it. In its erotic and scatological conceits, the novel brings poles together: nature and civilization, Harlem and Texas, renewal and waste. Writing in the headlong disc-jockey language of teenagers, Mailer, outrageous comedian, serves also as seer. Here language—spoof, rhyme, and pun—explode into dirge or song.

In some critical circles, it is fashionable to say that Mailer has become the genius journalist of the age. The opinion is based on his later works: *The Armies of the Night* (1968), about the protest march on the Pentagon; *Miami and the Siege of Chicago* (1968), about the Republican and Democratic Presidential Conventions; *Of a Fire on the Moon* (1971), about the first moon landing; and *The Prisoner of Sex* (1971), about literature, eroticism and Women's Lib. But the opinion is tendentious. The usual categories of fiction and fact, novel and history, autobiography and polemic often break down in recent literature. Furthermore, the imagination of Mailer, transcending the mock heroics of his egoism, compels events to yield a complex sense of human destiny.

No American writer, striking through posture and mask, transforms radical knowledge of the Self into forms more bright and amazing, or claims so much for the awareness of men in our time.

PROMINENT NOVELISTS

Wright Morris

One of the earliest novelists to emerge on the postwar scene, Wright Morris (born 1910) provides in his work a

link between two eras of fiction. He harks back to Sinclair
Lewis and Sherwood Anderson and also foreshadows the
sophisticated humor and anxieties of a generation younger
than his own. Solitary, prolific, enjoying fitfully public acclaim, laboring more often in obscurity, he seeks to repossess
American reality by penetrating its past, stripping its myths.
Morris is native to the plains of Nebraska; his characters, frail,
inward people, return to their Midwestern past in order to
find some viable identity of their own.

His novels vary in quality. Some seem opaque, tedious, or
frivolous; a few attain permanent distinction. Certainly Morris
is an artist; conscious of his material, he struggles continually
against its flatness. In his brilliant study *The Territory Ahead*
(1958) he examines the native tradition of Cooper, Hawthorne, Melville, Twain, James, Faulkner, Hemingway, con-
cluding that the myths of the receding frontier serve both
as help and hindrance in the writer's task. Of his own predicament, he says: "Too much ore. The hopper of my green
and untrained imagination was both nourished and handi-
capped by it." No doubt, this prompts him to devise a style,
laconic, oblique in its sense of person, place, and time, by
which he hopes to refine the facts and fancies of America
into some expression that would serve as his own discovered
identity. So often, however, his sense of the particular, of
people and human quiddity, leaves no impression of depth
on the mind.

Yet, from his first autobiographical novel, *My Uncle Dudley*
(1942), through more than a dozen works, Morris tries to
impose the field of his inner vision on fragments of experience. Certain characters recur, particularly the boy in that
first novel who becomes the seeking consciousness of later
fictions; the entanglements of familial relations move back
and forth in time through the peculiar aura of style. Isolation, silence, memory, and above all the muteness or failure
of love, the inability to respond, are the concerns of his best

work. Like Anderson before him, Morris records the ordeals of the passionate life in country and town, woman's incapacity to give of herself, the pathos of man's dream. Thus in *Man and Boy* (1951), *The Works of Love* (1952), *The Deep Sleep* (1953), *The Huge Season* (1954), *The Field of Vision* (1956), and *Ceremony in Lone Tree* (1960), he pursues the American Self among debris of love and recollection.

Ceremony in Lone Tree is typical, a chatty elegy of Nebraskan life, embracing four generations of Scanlons, located in the ghost towns of the plains. The violent present intrudes in references to the atomic bomb exploded in nearby Nevada, or in the mass killings perpetrated by two adolescents who go on the rampage—"I want to be somebody," says one, and "I got tired of being pushed around," says the other. Beneath the humor and triviality of relatives, men and women cheat themselves of existence, and evil lurks in childish places. When old Tom Scanlon, who knew Buffalo Bill, dies on the eve of his ninetieth birthday, the ceremony at Lone Tree ends without really ending the peculiar stiffness and solitude of that country.

Satire and nostalgia mingle in Morris's work. However, in such later fictions as *What a Way to Go* (1962), a kind of lightness, an amusing triviality, begins to show. Hoping to catch the new mood of erotic comedy, he shifts his focus; his locale ranges from Italy to Mexico. But his lasting contribution lies elsewhere. Trained initially as a photographer, Morris composes in his best novels a montage of static scenes through which the lost life of Americans may be glimpsed.

Bernard Malamud

Though critics still differ in assigning Bernard Malamud (born 1914) a precise place in the Jewish school of fiction, they rarely dispute his importance. His place is his own.

Obviously, he restores the Hebraic tradition to a brash new world. His work implies Yiddish lore, the wry and equivocal quality of the Jewish joke, the cadences of some immemorial speech. Malamud's lucid style, spare in pain, rich in sensuous inflections, carries Jewish conscience into our midst. Yet it is also clear that both his style and morality transcend the specific heritage of Judaism. "Jews," he says, "are absolutely the very *stuff* of drama"; and the purpose of the writer is "to keep civilization from destroying itself." Thus the heroes of Malamud become, no less than the author himself, symbols of struggling humanity, partaking in its ambiguous fate.

The heroes of Malamud, usually ordinary and solitary people, so gracelessly human, conform superficially to the image of the *schlemiel-schlimazel*. Yet they serve to affirm the possibilities of dignity for all; prisoners of circumstance, they still find the means of regeneration. This is Malamud's abiding theme—conversion, moral rebirth—which sustains his humanism in an age inward with the various terrors of apocalypse. Suffering makes for laughter as it makes for truth, and truth, acting on the heart, renews the whole man. The density of social facts in Malamud's fiction may, in the mind of some readers, awaken memories of the proletarian novels of the Thirties. But the facts of Malamud are not prescriptive, and his characters translate themselves continually from social scapegoats to mythic redeemers. Thus, his vision comprises myth and actuality, the spirit's freedom and the weight of the world; trust and irony are part of his single craft.

Malamud's first novel, *The Natural* (1952), receives belated recognition. Obscure in parts and original in conception, it comes slowly into focus in the larger pattern of his fiction. The story enmeshes the life of a modern baseball hero, Roy Hobbs, into various legendary patterns. Heavily overlaid with symbols, the work evokes the popular mystique of baseball, the Horatio Alger paradigm of success, Homeric tales,

Arthurian quest motifs, and ancient vegetation rites. The snappy slang of sport and the sacred archetypes of tradition come together. In betraying the ideal code of baseball and rejecting the love of a true woman, Hobbs shows no sense of "something over and above earthly things." Primary as is Malamud's theme, his method remains open to questions. How integral is the mythic structure to the purpose of the book? How congenial is its grotesque tone to the author himself?

None of these questions occur in reading *The Assistant* (1957). Here Malamud develops the theme of spiritual conversion in flawless form. Set in a milieu of immigrant shopkeepers and minority groups, the novel transforms downbeat city streets into some drab version of pastoral, into a discrete myth of renascence. The heaviness of poverty or ignorance, the alienation of the Jew in a land of Gentiles, the violence of unformed desire, the persistence of hope, inform the love story of Frank Alpine and Helen Bober. The Bobers toil sixteen hours a day in a grocery store, barely eking out a living; this is their share of the American Dream. But their daughter, Helen, reads in the library and holds out for a better fate. Into their midst comes "the assistant," Frank, to whom pain is familiar though still unintelligible. An Italian among Jews, Frank discovers himself slowly, purgation in humility, regeneration through love and sacrifice. He suffers circumcision, becomes after Passover a Jew. Without sentimentality, the novel engages the harsh, contradictory stuff of existence. Its luminous metaphors, its clear rhythms, speak beyond irony, beyond inconclusiveness, of human responsibility.

Two collections of stories, *The Magic Barrel* (1958) and *Idiots First* (1963) follow. These contain some of the best as well as the poorest fiction of Malamud. The best usually deal with Jewish material—"The Magic Barrel," "Take Pity," "The Mourners," "Idiots First," "The Last Mohican"—the worst, set abroad, have a glossy quality.

There is little gloss in *A New Life* (1961). Somewhat forced, somewhat secondhand in its felt life, the book centers on a faintly sour academic, S. Levin, who leaves New York City streets in search of fuller possibilities in the Far West (Oregon?). Topical references to politics—the Korean War, McCarthyism, American Democracy—and social satire abound; but the turning point comes when Levin discovers his love for Pauline Gilley, the wife of a colleague. This is no great romantic love. It is a love born of some unacknowledged imperative, sustained by irony, a willed commitment. At the end, when Levin leaves with Pauline and all of her adopted children, he does so toward an uncertain destiny.

The Fixer (1966) suggests a far more frightening and splendid destiny for man. Drawing freely on an incident of Jewish persecution—the trial of Mendel Beiliss, accused in Kiev, 1913, of the "ritual murder" of a Christian child—the work distills history into a parable of terror and absurdity resisted to the last. Yakov Bok, a poor and frail fixer, pits himself against the legacy of human despotism to insist on his innocence. Thus, he restores to all men not merely justice or dignity but a place, a meaning, in the universe. Bok will settle only for the largest questions. "Who invented my life?" he asks. Tormented in solitary confinement, he struggles with his tsarist tormentors, with his Jewish heritage, with his God. Querulous, impotent, quixotic, this minimal hero finally emerges from a prison into which all men are born. With harrowing control, Malamud guides the story of his fixer to an end that is perhaps too abrupt. The language at once sears and sings. The process of continuous genocide that we call history finds in this novel both a challenge and a response.

There are, of course, comic and grotesque touches in *The Fixer*. These become rather inept in *Pictures of Fidelman* (1969). Cracked, funny, and often frivolous, the various episodes refract the attempts of Fidelman to justify his existence in the mirror of his failed art. Only in the last episode, "Glass

Blower of Venice," does he remake his world with a deeper sensual knowledge of himself. The work, one feels, adds little to the stature of Malamud.

The figure of the artist becomes more richly symbolic in *The Tenants* (1971), symbolic of the contemporary "occluded self." In a crumbling house, deserted by all except two fanatic writers, Lesser and Spearmint, one a Jew, the other Black, a spectral drama of art, sex, and race is played out. Locked in his own sense of fate, each destroys life around him, painfully destroying himself. The complex hostility of Jew and Black assumes other oppositions between form and energy, art and politics, self-hatreds of various kinds. Without carrying his themes to a new level of insight, Malamud displays both tact and tensity in the writing of this book, a novel, elliptic style blending narrative and dream. The point of view shifts in the shadowy symbolic space of a tenement waiting for the wreckers' ball while the various authors write their way to death. Inconclusively, the novel suggests alternate ends of itself.

On the whole, Malamud is not an experimentalist in fiction. His genius is not expansive, his moral imagination almost too steadfast. Still, in his rigorous art, he gives to the Jew a deep-hued definition in American society. Above all a humanist, affirmative beneath all ambiguities, Malamud aspires to recover justice and decency in the world, to recover the human measure of universal things, and to embrace the spirit's renewal.

J. D. Salinger

The meteoric career of J. D. Salinger (born 1919) seems to end in silence and voluntary obscurity. There is a time in the early postwar years when his stories, deft and teasing, satisfy the needs of a youthful generation opposed to the

spiritual vulgarity of their culture. Collected in *Nine Stories*
(1953), the best of these narratives portray children or
adolescents, various misfits in middle-class suburbia, who
long for simplicity and truth. Their longing expresses itself
in tender or bitter quixotic gestures; the gestures suggest
something beyond satire or sentimentality. Already, social
motive begins to yield to religious insight; and the discursive
irony of squalor gives way to the wordless impulse of love
as we move from "Down at the Dinghy" and "Uncle Wiggily
in Connecticut" to "For Esmé—With Love and Squalor" and
"De Daumier-Smith's Blue Period."

But it is in Salinger's single novel, *The Catcher in the Rye*
(1951), that the period finds its testament of loss. The hero
Holden Caulfield, a fugitive prep school student with red
hunting cap askew, roams New York City encountering only
mendacity and phoniness. He ends in a sanatorium, from
which he recounts, in the first person, his tale, tangy with
the colloquial idiom of hurt adolescence. Like Huck Finn,
this latter-day picaresque refuses civilization; but unlike his
tough predecessor, Holden discovers no "territory ahead,"
only madness within. But madness is also the measure of his
responsiveness. Holden fights with bullies, gives money away
to nuns, rubs out obscenities from school walls, wonders
where the ducks of Central Park go when their pond is frozen.
He reads the notebook of a child all day and into the night.
When his little sister Phoebe asks him what he would like
to do as a grown-up, Holden muses on Robert Burns's song,
"If a body meet a body coming through the rye." Then he
answers: "I keep picturing all these kids playing some game
in this big field of rye and all. Thousands of little kids, and
nobody's around—nobody big, I mean—except me. And I'm
standing at the edge of some crazy cliff. . . . And that's all
I'd do all day. I'd just be the catcher in the rye and all."
Humor, irony, and wistfulness barely conceal the sadness of
city life, the equivocations of society, the reign of solitude.

The novel mocks hypocrisy, egoism, compromise, and also comes close to sounding the note of dread. But whimsy and slapstick keep terror at bay; and Holden, though he can love only his sister Phoebe, retains the saving grace of vulnerability.

With time, the religious interests of Salinger—in Zen Buddhism, in primitive Christianity—deepen. A sacramental sense of existence, coy at first, clearly asserts itself. And language, the very pride of the artist, begins to move toward silence. The evidence is in the later novellas, which reflect the extraordinary Glass family in a mirror darkly. *Franny and Zooey* (1961) and *Raise High the Roofbeam, Carpenters, and Seymour: An Introduction* (1963) astonish the critics with their prolix and convoluted shapes, their digressions and asides. In them, Salinger shatters the story form into countless fragments: speeches, letters, diaries, footnotes, telephone conversations, messages scrawled everywhere. It is as if his purpose to redeem the "desecrations" of language by parody and discontinuity could thus be attained. "No dependence upon words and letters" runs one of "The Four Statements" of Zen. The narrator of the last volume, Buddy Glass, a frank foil to Salinger himself, pretending to describe his matchless brother, Seymour, really aspires to quiet his own artistic will. And in the problematic suicide of Seymour, Buddy tries to see some reflection of his own life, of human destiny perhaps. For Seymour (See-more) offers more than artifice. "I say that the true artist-seer, the heavenly fool who can and does produce beauty, is mainly dazzled to death by his own scruples, the blinding shapes and colors of his own sacred human conscience," Buddy concludes.

Secluded for many years and nearly forgotten by a generation that once hung on his tales, Salinger ceases to write. The parodist of suburbia becomes, like his own character, Seymour Glass, a kind of holy suicide. But his artistry in short fiction endures.

Kurt Vonnegut

Part satirist and part visionary, Kurt Vonnegut (born 1922) enjoys a sudden vogue since the late Sixties, particularly among youths disaffected with militarism, greed, and excessive rationality, with various ecological and technological disasters. A dark comedian even more than a satirist, Vonnegut expresses his rage, guilt, and compassion, his sense of being alive in a world of death, in frightening dystopias. But as sly prophet, he presents alternatives to the human condition in science fictions, disporting the virtues of his favorite Tralfamadorians. His urgency carries itself lightly in fantasy or whimsy, though his gruff sentimentality also tends to weaken his hold on complex realities. Somewhat typically, he says: "And I realize now that the two main themes of my novels were stated by my siblings: 'Here I am cleaning shit off practically everything' and 'No pain.'" A personalist, he translates his redemptive dream into cute language.

Player Piano (1952), minatory and somewhat uninspired, deals with an anti-utopia run by computers, ruled by high-IQ engineers, a managerial society of boredom and conformity. But revolution finally comes to Illium with the help of a disillusioned leader, Paul Proteus, and the discontented mass of "Reeks and Wrecks."

In *The Sirens of Titan* (1959), however, Vonnegut creates a witty galactic fantasy, exposing the warped purpose of the planet Earth, and envisioning the mystery of the Universal Will To Become. Thus the richest Earthling, Malachi Constant, undertakes his quest in space, experiences various metamorphoses, and learns from Salo, the Tralfamadorian, about "hypnotic anarchy" as well as love. "It took us that long to realize that a purpose of human life, no matter who is controlling it, is to love whoever is around to be loved,"

Constant concludes. Thus, for Vonnegut, love remains an aspect of cosmic determinism.

The element of fantasy is controlled in Vonnegut's most complex work, *Mother Night* (1961, 1966). A study of contemporary nihilism and totalitarianism, of pretense become reality, the novel explores the psyche of an American Nazi, Howard Campbell, Jr., a double agent, through many reversals, through his search for conscience and being. The insane discrepancies between private and public worlds, the nature of evil, "hatred without limit," the loss of will—all come into question. Written in the confessional mode by Campbell himself, the work reveals a "man who served evil too openly and good too secretly, the crime of his times."

With *Cat's Cradle* (1963), however, Vonnegut returns to fantasy in an apocalyptic confrontation between science and religion, between facts or fictions of a different kind: "the heartbreaking necessity of lying about reality, and the heartbreaking impossibility of lying about it." The book develops its own cultist language, which includes "Bokononism," the religion of harmless untruths, "karass," "granfalloon," and so forth. Less notable, *God Bless You, Mr. Rosewater* (1965) mingles dadaist play and social satire; and *Welcome to the Monkey House* (1968) includes some slick and trivial stories as well as a few inventive pieces.

It is with *Slaughterhouse-Five* (1969) that Vonnegut gains widest acclaim. Centering on an awful event, the fire-bombing of Dresden during World War II—the author survives the event as a prisoner of war hiding in the cold meat lockers beneath a slaughterhouse—the book unites realism and science fiction, accusation and exorcism, terror and love, in somewhat autobiographical form. Here is a spare description of the devastated city: "There were hundreds of corpse mines operating by and by. They didn't smell bad at first, were wax museums. But then the bodies rotted and liquefied, and the stink was like roses and mustard gas. So it goes."

So it goes: death everywhere, accident, mystery, outrage. This is Vonnegut's song, echoing in the depths of his nostalgia. A fatalist and dreamer, he conceals his discomforts within strange levity. His harshest critics find him lacking in mind. Yet Vonnegut offers, more than levity, an honest perception of his moment; and creates a style both lax and gnomic, "telegraphic schizophrenic," which attempts to carry his sense of discontinuity toward some visionary end.

James Purdy

Violence and nostalgia, those twin forces of American literature, converge once more in the work of James Purdy (born 1923). A native of Ohio, he evolves a unique style, deceptively simple, which vaguely recalls Kafka as well as Sherwood Anderson. His humor, black, surreal, disguises the world of violated innocence; gothic terror and arcadian dream sustain the tension of his imagination. Somewhere at the center of that imagination, an erotic intuition of life—of love and its strange betrayals, of the vagaries of desire—takes hold. Bitterly opposed to materialism and conformity in America, he creates allegorical fantasies that celebrate children, pariahs, and perverts, the spiritual ache of wayward individuals.

His first collection, comprising eleven stories and a novella, called *The Color of Darkness* (1957), receives due recognition in England before America. Concise, masterly in absurd dialogue as in dramatic suggestion, both diabolic and tender, the stories render the intolerable ambiguities of love and loneliness. The novella, entitled "63: Dream Palace," stands among the best and most harrowing things written by Purdy. A later collection of stories and short plays, *Children Is All* (1962), confirms the skill of Purdy in expressing hypnotically what his characters, trapped in fear or guilt, can hardly permit themselves to express.

But it is in *Malcolm* (1959) that Purdy finds the scope of his extraordinary vision. Describing the encounters of a fatherless youth with various cruel or grotesque figures, the novel spins a comic parable of initiation into the modern world, a world loveless and void. Malcolm is the exploited innocent abroad, managing to preserve his innocence, speaking always the truth; but he is also as a "cypher . . . a blank," around which human rapacity takes shape. Malcolm is the still center; for as he confesses to Girard, he hardly feels that he exists. Purdy's satire illumines an outlandish portrait gallery: an astrologer, an undertaker, a midget, a *grande dame*, an ex-burgler, a famous chanteuse, among others. Too young, unschooled, unprepared for life, nothing remains for Malcolm but to marry the voracious Melba. But marriage, "which ushers most people into life, in Malcolm's case . . . ushered him into happiness—and death." With his death, consumed as it were by the passion of these others, the circle breaks. After some gossip concerning Malcolm's resurrection, he is quite forgotten by everyone. The world of the novel is one of twilight, "with a coolness too, like perpetual autumn, an autumn that will not pass into winter owing to some damage perhaps to the machinery of the cosmos."

The Nephew (1960), by contrast, favors a more realistic mode; it shares a partial fidelity to the Midwestern scene with a later work, *Jeremy's Version* (1970). Both picture small-town American life with acid sympathy. Both seek to penetrate rumor and sentiment among townspeople and to gain some insight into primary human relations. *The Nephew*, compact and modulated, offers such an insight into the life of two elderly people, eschewing the fussiness that mars *Jeremy's Version*.

Two other works of the Sixties reveal Purdy in full possession of his powers. *Cabot Wright Begins* (1964) mocks the outrageous falsity of contemporary culture. Its sly treatment of various New York characters, among them the cheerful rape artist, Cabot Wright, adapts the pornographic manner to social criticism. More tragic, *Eustace Chisolm and the Works* (1967) explores Purdy's perennial theme, love disturbed, with an intensity nearly religious. Set in Chicago of the mid-Thirties, the novel traces the fate of various misfits and outsiders through the Depression ending with the war. But the center of the tale is erotic torment; and the climax uniting Private Haws and Captain Stadger in an army camp unites also politics and sex in terror. For Eustace Chisolm himself, would-be poet, survival requires him to shed the illusions of his art and to accept another reality. Quoting Dryden, Chisolm defines it:

> I know thee, Love! in deserts thou wert bred,
> And at the dugs of savage Tigers fed;
> Alien of birth, usurper of the plains!

Purdy's voice can be querulous; his world can be too cramped, its blackness almost willed; and women seldom bring life or grace into it. But he understands the inner chaos of men too well, the archetypal night of their souls. Like some absurd lapidary or icy expressionist, he cuts the lineaments of dread and innocence into the gross matter of existence.

Truman Capote

Among postwar American writers, few come to be known so young as Truman Capote (born 1924). There is no elegant way to summarize his work. His styles vary too much, though style itself remains a central part of his achievement. Born and raised in the Deep South, his earliest fiction develops some mannerisms of the region. Yet the legacy of Faulkner affects Capote in a peculiar way, less gothic than exotic, less elemental than oneiric. An ethereal sexuality, often homo-erotic, suffuses his fiction. Nor does the Southern manner cling to him for long. There is the crackling travelogue, from Ischia to Haiti, of *Local Color* (1950). There is the hilarious account of a trip to Russia, with the cast of *Porgy and Bess*, in *The Muses Are Heard* (1956). There is the New York or Kansas setting of his later novels.

As the locale of Capote's work changes, so the forms of his fiction open. His preciosity gives way to social curiosity, to the zany humor of, say, his film script, *Beat the Devil*. Behind the frills and fashions of his prose, one senses the tenacity of some purpose. It is as if the solitary gaze of Narcissus, watery, vague, could in time sharpen enough to discern contours of reality rising beneath the surface.

As early as in the first stories of Capote, collected in *A Tree of Night* (1949), a distinction may be observed between his nocturnal and daylight styles. A sense of dread attends the "instant of petrified violence," the locked dream, the disin-tegrating psyche, in such stories as "Miriam," "The Headless Hawk," "A Tree of Night." Yet if terror and the preternatural define the nocturnal mode, comedy and social manners char-acterize the daylight view of "My Side of the Matter," "Jug of Silver," "Children on Their Birthdays." The tone is chatty, admits of first-person anecdotes; and the characters engage concrete realities in a small Southern town rather than ab-stract horrors in a Northern metropolis.

Capote's first two novels heighten this contrast, though both are still romances, that "neutral territory," Hawthorne once said, "somewhere between the real world and fairy-land, where the Actual and the Imaginary may meet, and each imbue itself with the nature of the other." *Other Voices, Other Rooms* (1948) remains a tour de force of the dark, mythic sensibility that the Southern formalist critics help to make fashionable in the Forties and early Fifties. The book enfolds the reader in its poetic language, original and also overwrought, enfolds him in an inscape of fright and perversion. The action centers on the boy, Joel Knox, whose initiation leads him through many mysteries to the spectral Cloud Hotel, where he is finally confirmed in his identity. The quest for the Other—be he god, father, seducer, or mirror image—ends in a hallucination of self-knowledge, a vision of love, loneliness, and mutability. Set also in the South, *The Grass Harp* (1951) deals more humorously with the end of boyhood innocence, and its tone is far less eerie than nostalgic. As Collier Fenwick hears the voice of the wind through a field of Indian grass, he recalls a crisis of his youth among elderly women, besieged in a tree house by the wicked World, which must storm the simple Heart. Yet song and memory redeem Fenwick's present and adult realities by releasing the impulses of love.

Here ends the Southern phase of Capote's fiction. A new kind of whimsy, or Camp, affects his next work, *Breakfast at Tiffany's* (1958), set mainly in New York, which celebrates headlong Holly Golightly. Bittersweet in its naïve abandon, current with chic *argot*, the narrative, a kind of lipstick picaresque, suggests the interest of the times in open forms. Thus, the bruised innocence of Holden Caulfield returns in Holly, who is more frivolous but also more free.

Less than a decade later, Capote once again changes his role. We see him *In Cold Blood* (1966) as herald of a new genre, the "non-fiction novel," which recognizes the convergence of fiction and fact in times of outrage, the insane surrealism of daily life. Based upon accounts of grisly Kansas murders of a wealthy farmer and his entire family, the book finally raises vast questions about American society, the anger and deprivation of men, the workings of justice. With covert art, Capote compels years of research, mounds of tapes and notes, endless interviews, into form; he selects, organizes, juxtaposes; he draws nets of animal imagery around his characters, and manages to keep the violence controlled. His sympathy for stunted life quickens the work with life of its own. The fierce controversy that greets the book centers on two issues: the authenticity of the "non-fiction" form as a medium of narrative, and the authenticity of the author in his uneasy personal relation to the two killers, waiting execution on death row.

Capote survives controversy, though he may not thrive on it as Mailer does. He has endurance as well as wit. He projects many roles of himself—the aesthete, the terrorist, the humorist, the jet-setter, the social critic—and his mastery of language is clear. Yet, with the possible exception of *In Cold Blood*, he fails to provide the age with some compelling reflection of itself.

John Hawkes

Once again, the gothic strain, filtering through the work of so many writers of the period, becomes almost the principle of design in the fiction of John Hawkes (born 1925). Faulkner, Djuna Barnes, and Nathanael West contribute to the bizarre poetic sensibility of Hawkes, and his admiration for Flannery O'Connor is known. The satirical impulse in him objectifies, even as it burlesques, the "terrifying similarity between the unconscious desires of the solitary man and the disruptive needs of the visible world." The malice of familiar objects, the terror of love gone coldly mad, the fascination of unstated evil, the ancestral magic of death or disease hold his fiction in surreal fixity. Yet the surrealism of Hawkes is precise. He wants to discern the "small product of the huge phenomenon," the "wounds in the form of fungi," which we all "suffer any summer or winter afternoon." For this purpose, Hawkes develops a personal idiom which blurs experience but makes inner life preternaturally clear. He says: "Between the contemporary poem and experimental novel, there is not so much an alliance as merely the sharing of a birthmark: both come from the same place and are equally disfigured at the start."

His first book, *The Cannibal* (1949), is a war novel that departs completely from the naturalistic conventions of that genre. It is an allegory of cyclical crime and retribution set in occupied Germany, compressing the military events of 1870, 1914, and 1945 into grisly archetypes: murder, madness, and cannibalism. Various characters embody the ritual of victim and executioner, who recapitulate the history of the human race. In their violence, atavism and absurdity meet; the private and public worlds collapse. The style, menacing and macabrely humorous, creates a climate of ancient decay. "The undertaker had no more fluid for his corpses; the town nurse grew old and fat on no food at all. By mistake, some drank from poisoned wells. Banners were in the mud. . . . " In Hawkes's stories and novellas—*Charivari* (1950), *The Goose on the Grave* (1954), *The Owl* (1954)— the insidious climate persists even when social and dramatic content tends to fade.

Hawkes finds new subjects for his subsequent novels though his angle of vision remains the same. *The Lime Twig* (1961), set in England, evokes a mythical world of power and evil in the racing underworld. Behind the faces of Hencher, or Larry, or Margaret, a peculiar dream takes place; the beauties of degradation, the horrors of incompletion, the travesties of annihilation haunt their sleep. In a world without justice or necessity, Hawkes says, "there is no pathetic fun or mournful frolic like our desire, the consummation of the sparrow's wings."

Second Skin (1964) brings more light into Hawkes's world. The New England coast, rocks, cloudy sun, and sea reflect the texture of cruelty, of desire, reflect the endurance of Skipper, the narrator, who refuses to partake in the doom of his heritage. The complex action moves back and forth in time, from the Pacific to New York to Maine, comprising lovers and enemies, ending with Skipper's evasion of death. Here the sentences link; the novel, more than a collection of images and rhythms, coheres. Hawkes surmounts his innate weakness: a language, though original, too retrogressive and discrete, defying the broader synthesis of experience. Something akin to a synthesis is implicit in the last words of Skipper: "Because now I am fifty-nine years old and I knew I would be, and now there is the sun in the evening, the moon at dawn, the still voice. That's it. The sun in the evening. The moon at dawn. The still voice."

The insistent lyrical voice of Hawkes makes itself heard once more in *The Blood Oranges* (1971), his most exoteric work. The story, set perhaps in some Grecian seaside place called by the mythical name of Illyria, concerns two couples, Cyril and Fiona, Hugh and Catherine, who dance to the ancient music of desire and death. Cyril, the narrator, the driving force of the action, thinks of himself as a "sex-singer," doing "Love's will" in all its polymorphous perversities. Yet the erotic subtleties of the novel, the very motives of the characters, seem in the end merely aspects of poetic virtuosity, echoes of an authorial voice sounding in the mind.

Gifted intensely, John Hawkes carries poetic fiction as far as it can go, retaining still a strong semblance of the old form. He does not question his narrow art, nor range wide in the emotions of men.

William Styron

A Virginian by birth, William Styron (born 1925) begins his literary career writing in the Southern manner; soon thereafter, he shows an independent sensibility. His work, brilliant in parts, shifting from rhetoric to sudden poetry, dramatically rich, seeks between violence and ambiguity some definition of personal integrity. The search often fails because Styron seems to lack a felt attitude toward life, a distinctive power of evaluation.

The influence of Faulkner and Fitzgerald appears in Styron's first novel, *Lie Down in Darkness* (1951). Yet the book also harks back to the baroque tradition of John Donne and Sir Thomas Browne; invokes Freud; and still remains Styron's most vivid, most personal, expression. The novel presents a Southern family locked in a domestic tragedy; love wears the face of guilt or incest, and the search for childhood innocence leads only to self-destruction. Through Peyton, doomed, lovely daughter of the Loftis family, the author makes his symbolic statement on the decay of the South—manners with few morals, dissolving community, fake religiosity—and on the larger trials of the modern world. As Peyton puts it to a contemporary: "Those people back in the Lost Generation. Daddy I guess. . . . They thought they were lost. They were crazy. They weren't lost. What they were doing was losing us." Still, though the characters lie down in darkness, Styron's art burns their ashes into light.

Styron's later novels expand his range; seldom shoddy or trite, they do not burn, however, so incandescently. *The Long March* (1952) depicts a Marine camp realistically. The hero, Captain Mannix, awkward and unwilling rebel, dramatizes the issue of conformity so nagging in the early Fifties. *Set This House on Fire* (1960), a work less esteemed in America than in Europe, where the action takes place, explores the existential themes of alienation and murderous freedom. Its protagonist, the expatriate Cass Kinsolving, ends by finding his manhood in a provisional choice of being over nothingness. Melodramatic, sometimes glib in its use of current ideas, the novel still shows authentic dramatic power in certain scenes.

The most controversial, perhaps the most ambitious, of Styron's novels, *The Confessions of Nat Turner* (1967), purports to be a "meditation on the history" of a nineteenth-century slave rebellion in Virginia. The event, of course, presages the contemporary Black Movement in America. Written in a sequence of dreams, reflections, and actions, mostly from the point of view of the Negro rebel Nat Turner himself, the book raises complex issues of literary and historical authenticity. Black militants, in particular, register many objections, ranging from the "voice" of the work to its "veracity." Bold in conception, tense and moving in some sections, the novel, nevertheless, avoids the deepest insights of its subject.

Despite his gifts—social flair, a novelistic instinct, language that can sing—Styron does not reckon completely with his special intuition. Something in his imagination seems to inhibit its own originality.

John Barth

John Barth (born 1930) clearly belongs to the small number of American authors who carry their experiments to the limits of fiction, the edge of silence. A master of contradictions, an intimate of the void, Barth knows how to turn the crisis of language and form to his own advantage. In a signal essay, "The Literature of Exhaustion," he says of the new writer: "His artistic victory . . . is that he confronts an intellectual dead end and employs it against itself to accomplish new human work." Older writers, such as Borges, Beckett, or Nabokov, strike us as virtuosos of "exhaustion," and others younger still than Barth—say Thomas Pynchon or Donald Barthelme—carry the tradition forward.

The skeptical temper of Barth, his parodic genius—which collapses sometimes in puerile humor—are evident through-

out his fiction. Intuitively, he understands the existential
mummery of our time. Instinctively, he finds the given social
or phenomenal world arbitrary, faintly ludicrous. In an inter-
view, he admits: "My argument is with the facts of life, not
the conditions of it. . . . I'm not very responsible in the
Social Problems way, I guess." Increasingly, Barth wants to
inhabit the region of "Ultimacy," which lies beyond irony
and fancy, in some pure self-delighting realm of the verbal
mind. Like many artists before him, he insists on artifice in
art. Yet, like them too, he becomes a moralist by indirection.
His characters often suffer from mirror gazing, or from "cos-
mopsis," an excess of consciousness; what they must learn,
slowly, after many painful travesties of the flesh, is that life
can justify itself and love can justify man.

The first two novels of Barth have a certain wry energy,
though their structures still conform to the conventions of
fiction. *The Floating Opera* (1956, 1967) declares his abiding
theme: the uninvolved life "lived by the heartbeat," in total
absense of intrinsic values, cerebral and null. The complexity
of the story depends less on its sexual imbroglios, to which
Barth will return, than on its self-questioning point of view.
The narrative conveys the paradox of Todd Andrews who
contemplates suicide, caught between reason and instinct,
voice and silence; and it further suggests the paradox of his
author, who makes art of a nihilistic theme. Full of feints
and asides, the novel seeks to justify itself in comic terms.

The clue, then, is the play of narrative, the story in itself,
as *The End of the Road* (1958, 1967) again shows. Once
more, the anti-hero skirmishes with the endless possibilities
of existence, achieves immobility. "In a sense," he says, "I
am Jacob Horner"; and mindlessly we add, "Who sat in a
corner." Jake, child of multiplicities, has run out of motives.
He takes two healers, one to instruct him in arbitrary rules,
the other in continuous performances. They fail to give necessity to his choices. Embroiled also in a sexual triangle, Horner

senses how close the nihilistic self of our time stands to the end of the road. He saves himself from complete oblivion by attaching himself to his author. "Articulation!" he cries. "*There*, by Jove, was my absolute, if I could be said to have one. . . . To turn experience into speech. . . . "

In subsequent novels, Barth accepts his self-parodic role even more exuberantly, giving us, he says, works that "imitate the form of the Novel, by an author who imitates the role of Author." *The Sot-Weed Factor* (1960, 1967) is certainly as prodigious in length as it is farcical in metaphysics. The work calls into question all things—the mystery of human personality, the antics of love, the madness of history, the surrealism of nature—in the form of eighteenth-century gothic and picaresque narratives. It is a pastiche of various styles, straining the limits of credibility in plot and devious subplot. Ostensibly, the author wants to recount the story of another author, Ebenezer Cooke, who actually published in 1708 a poem entitled "The Sot-Weed Factor" (early American for tobacco merchant). Yet the sum of history for both authors appears "no more than the stuff of metaphors"; therefore, everything is permitted. Characters shift or exchange their realities; and in the bawdy play of appearances, Englishman and American, Paleface and Indian, Catholic and Protestant, Hero and Villain, Man and Woman flicker across the screen of language. Yet, despite itself, this slapstick epic of Colonial Maryland becomes an allegory of radical innocence in quest of a "seamless universe," an allegory, too, of the artist at the end of his tether. Thus, Cooke's tutor, Burlingame, that strange, self-creating genius of the novel who seems so often to speak for and against Barth, cries: "I am a Suitor of Totality, Embracer of Contradictories, Husband to all Creation, the Cosmic Lover!"

Pushing farrago and indeterminacy still farther, Barth creates in *Giles Goat-Boy* (1966) a rather more self-conscious allegory of all the destructive wisdom of the twentieth cen-

tury. Letters, forewords, and disclaimers enclose the main
narrative in equivocal frames; literary and topical references
abound in disorder, as if strewn by some berserk computer
that, Barth hints, may be the true author of the book. Pre-
sumably, one J. B., an academic novelist, puts aside his
favorite project concerning the Cosmic Amateur in order
to reconstruct the story of the Grand Tutor, Giles Goat-Boy,
part Christ and part Pan. Giles struggles from his animal
innocence toward the salvation of our race, losing himself
often in the tragic labyrinth of human consciousness. In the
process, Giles jostles Paradox, batters the Unnamable; exhausted, he cries: "I let go, I let all go." Yet he does attain
complete being in the arms of his beloved Anastasia, within
the bowels of a monstrous computer, WESCAC. Thereafter,
Giles puts himself beyond the malice and enmities of the
mind: "For me, Sense and Nonsense lost their meaning on
a night twelve years four months ago, in WESCAC's
Belly. . . ." The reader, though, is free to balk at the immense panorama of travesty in the novel. However taut or
complex beneath, however ingenious erudite, or funny, the
book tends to pall.

The parodic rage of Barth finds new expression in the
stories of *Lost in the Fun House* (1968). Living voice, printed
work, and magnetic tape conspire to create a kind of aural
montage, a conceit of genres. The forms of fiction turn themselves inside out, shed their skin in search of a new life
(Barth's public readings from this collection are virtuoso
performances of intermedia). Thus, the narrative attempts
to swallow itself by the tail in "Anonymiad"; or vanishes
into concentric brackets of itself, like a Chinese box, in
"Menelaiad"; or comes to rest in the hovering silence of the
tale, the teller, and the told, in "Title." "What is there to say
at this late date?" a voice in that last piece asks. "Let me
think, I'm trying to think. Same old story. Or. Or? Silence."
The solipsist narrators of Beckett, droning their way to death,

come to mind. Fictions float toward further fictions; words drift like galactic dust. All that remains in *Lost in the Fun House* is some distant echo of humor, the valence of loss.

Barth wants to align himself with the great narrators of open or whimsical experience: the authors of the *Arabian Nights*, Boccaccio, Rabelais, Cervantes, Sterne. Yet Barth is of course much closer to Borges and Beckett, authors of silence in postmodern literature. His despair, however, seems lighter than theirs; his fabulations often more frivolous. He writes about murder, incest, and madness as if they had no resonance but in hollow laughter. Evasive and arch, teeth clenched, he prefers "Not To," in brilliant verbal games.

John Updike

John Updike (born 1932) shares the ironic temper, the lexical agility, of both Barth and Nabokov. His satiric focus, however, is narrower, his inventions less exuberant. He writes in a crisp, probing idiom, precise yet astonishing in imagery, sterile in an oddly poetic way. He chooses subtle middle-class characters who seldom suffer the extreme passions of their day. Updike, therefore, often seems a novelist of manners, a writer of clever sensibilities, deft up to a certain depth. Yet he also tries to sound some major themes—love, death, freedom, the burden of redemption in the contemporary world—in forms of some mythic resonance. Furthermore, because he declares himself a Christian, some admirers impute to him the theological interests of St. John of the Cross, Søren Kierkegaard, and Karl Barth. There is, of course, some dry dread in Updike's work, a fear of chaos and waste, a sense of the self's own emptiness; yet the dread remains most often locked in the detail.

The stories of *The Same Door* (1959), treating minor miseries and epiphanies in suburbia, demonstrate formal brilliance; and there is, more than brilliance, vibrancy in the later stories of *Pigeon Feathers* (1962). Updike's first novel, *The Poorhouse Fair* (1959), suggests similar lacks and promises. Set in a home for the elderly, it contrasts scientific with religious aspiration, the elimination of pain with that of evil. The poorhouse serves as a model of the future welfare state, benevolent and insensitive to the needs of mortal men. Intermittently, its crotchety inmates come alive humorously, ominously, as characters of a fiction.

Rabbit, Run (1960) is a work of greater power. "Rabbit" Angstrom represents the contradictory urges of the new hero to discover, beyond responsibility, beyond love even, a special fate for himself. Running from one failure to another, disengaging himself from the embroilments of sex, family, and society, he evades all corruptions but his own. Yet Rabbit remains alive to his spiritual quest; in the secular wasteland of the novel, he alone dramatizes the existential condition of man deprived of grace. Rightly inconclusive, the novel leaves the hero, dubiously mobile, with the feeling: "Goodness lies inside, there is nothing outside, those things he was trying to balance have no weight. He feels his inside as very real suddenly, a pure blank space in the middle of a dense net." The book manages to contain character, incident, and idea in a form without trickery or brittleness.

The form of *The Centaur* (1963) is denser and also more problematic. The novel reflects in the myth of Chiron the travails of a modern schoolteacher, Caldwell. As Chiron yields his immortality to expiate the sins of Prometheus, so does Caldwell accept death as a sacrifice to his artist son. The various levels of the story, mythic and realistic, allegorical and literal, collide in shifting perspectives, refracting degeneration, revealing death: "even at its immense stellar remove of impossibility, a grave and dreadful threat." The central assertion of the novel is that only "goodness" perdures. Profoundly moving in parts, merely clever or obscure in others, *The Centaur* seems the testimony of vast artistic ambitions partially fulfilled.

Of the Farm (1965), which takes place in Updike's native Pennsylvania, returns to straightforward narrative; so does *Couples* (1968), set in a small Eastern town, affluent and sexually frenetic. In both works, Woman—as mother and wife in one novel, as wife and mistress in the other—brings a special "presence," complicating in new ways the spiritual theme. Increasingly, Updike turns toward love as the mirror of human maladies. Yet his skill, evident in the earlier of these two books, fails in *Couples* to convey, beyond the intricacies of shuddering flesh, a biological or metaphysical meaning. Despite all its erotic permutations, the novel remains arid, tautological as a finite equation.

In *Rabbit Redux* (1971), however, Updike writes his most impressive novel. It is a sequel to the earlier work, showing us Harry Angstrom a decade later, flabbier, superficially more settled into a mediocre life, yet more fearful and confused than ever, therefore more alive and still spiritually on the run. Rabbit learns that all growth implies some kind of betrayal, that a man without force lacks the essential dignity of humanity. He loses his wife, his mistress, his house, his job; above all, he struggles with his illusion of the rightness and invincibility of America. What he discovers in himself is the mixed source of love and guilt, a new kind of strength. The book is determinedly topical, takes in the moon landing, the Vietnam war, the terrible discord of generations, the drugs and heedlessness of the counter-culture. And through the remarkable portait of Skeeter, it tries to reckon with the new Black consciousness. It is as if Updike wants to seize with compassion as good as his irony the center of disaster in the land, seize it so that he may endow his characters—Rabbit, or his wife Janice, or his mistress Jill, a teenage runaway from affluence, or Charlie Stavros, the car salesman who is Janice's lover—with life greater than their narrow souls can ever possess.

Updike can be too stingy and cerebral. At his worst, he lacks the courage of any large feeling. But his satire, as in *Bech: A Book* (1970), is adroit. And he sees more than the pretensions of society: he sees its spiritual vacuity. Though he conceals his arch themes—death, entropy, fear—they lend his best work inner tension and urgency.

TYPES AND TRENDS OF FICTION

The Short Story

The short story goes back to the nineteenth-century masters: Hawthorne and Poe, Crane and James. In the earlier part of the twentieth century, Anderson, Hemingway and Faulkner help to mold its character. In the postwar period, the short story, sharply defined by its scope and form, proves more resistant to various trends than the novel. It remains, nevertheless, popular. The mass market for newspapers, for magazines ranging from pulp to academic to avant-garde, makes story writing both lucrative and reputable.

It is no surprise, then, that a number of accomplished writers are first known for their short stories before the war ends. *The New Yorker* attracts authors of special wit and sensibility; *Story* shows greater variety in excellence; and the critical quarterlies, such as *Kenyon Review* and *Sewanee Review*, favor formalist structures. (Both *Story* and *Kenyon Review* are now defunct.) The best stories in the opinion of editors are collected each year in two anthologies: *Prize Stories: The O. Henry Awards* and *The Best American Short Stories of 19—*.

Very often, virtuosos of the short story are known as well for their longer fiction: J. D. Salinger, John Cheever, Flannery O'Connor, Bernard Malamud, Truman Capote, John Updike, James Purdy. But there are also writers whose achievement seems more intensely representative in the shorter form. J. F. Powers's *The Prince of Darkness, and Other Stories* (1947), Peter Taylor's *A Long Fourth, and Other Stories* (1948), and Jean Stafford's *Children Are Bored on Sunday* (1953) provide examples of that achievement in poignant decorum. Sedate as it may seem, the short story does evolve in the early Sixties. The lyric ceremonies of earlier decades give way to a rougher personal tone, as in R. V. Cassill's *The Father, and Other Stories* (1965), to violence, as in Alfred Chester's *Behold Goliath* (1964), or to absurdist humor, as in Donald Barthelme's *Come Back, Dr. Caligari* (1964).

The War Novel

It is natural that the war itself should provide young writers who have just climbed out of their uniforms with an experience large and troubling enough to compel the fictional imagination. Novelists of the generation of Hemingway and Dos Passos found in World War I a symbol of general collapse as well as personal disillusionment. But the next generation enters World War II with few illusions; and what they see in its unspeakable ravages seems to them not only the collapse of an old order but also a dread prophecy of the future. Senseless and efficient violence, the vast repression of everything human, alienation from self, society, and nature—these, the legacy of the war, threaten to define the condition of man in an age of totalitarianism or technocracy. Thus, the military life itself, the "war machine," comes to be viewed by writers like Norman Mailer and Joseph Heller as the microcosm of contemporary history; while others, like James Gould Cozzens and Herman Wouk, more cautious, try to distinguish between authority and tyranny.

On closer inspection, however, war fiction reveals great variety in theme, manner, and quality. The conflict between officers and enlisted men, the contrast between American and European or Oriental women, the character of the American soldier in war and peace, the meaning of courage, love, or death recur as issues. John Hersey's *A Bell for Adano* (1944), John Horne Burns's *The Gallery* (1947), Irwin Shaw's *The Young Lions* (1948), Norman Mailer's *The Naked and the Dead* (1948), Herman Wouk's *The Caine Mutiny* (1951), and James Jones's *From Here to Eternity* (1951)—of these the works of Burns, Mailer, and Jones stand out—suggest also that realism tends to prevail in the earliest war fictions. In Mailer's novel, however, there is already some hint of another, surrealistic form, reminiscent of Don Passos; and in John Hawkes's *The Cannibal* (1949), Thomas Berger's *Crazy in Berlin* (1958), Joseph Heller's *Catch-22* (1961), and Kurt Vonnegut's *Slaughterhouse-Five* (1969), the form breaks open to reckon with the deepening absurdities of the age.

Yet the most representative author of war fiction is perhaps James Jones (born 1921). His first novel, *From Here to Eternity*, set in the Schofield Barracks of Hawaii just before the attack on Pearl Harbor, movingly depicts the struggle of one soldier to maintain his identity, his dignity as a man. Private Robert E. Lee Prewitt, son of Harlan County, Kentucky, coal miners turned into a United States Army thirty-year man, defies the combined power of "the system" in the name of pride, pity, and justice, putting all human suffering into the clear, intolerable note of his bugle blowing Taps. The novel displays raw power and compassion, characters —Maggio, Fatso, Warden, Stark—stubborn in their vivid life, and a sense of outrage sustained in dramatic action and social fact.

"Men are killed by being always alike, always unremembered," Prewitt says; the same feeling informs Jones's novella, *The Pistol* (1958), which examines the nature of authority in its inevitable clash with personal "salvation." But it is in *The Thin Red Line* (1962) that Jones gives his fullest, his most technical account of the war. The "system" is no longer solely responsible for all human violations; men conspire through their lack of "realism" to defeat themselves. In the vast, murderous spectacle of jungle combat which Jones describes minutely, evil disguises itself as softness or illusion, as romantic heroism, as social cant that does not stand the test of natural survival. Thus, in Fife's initiation into combat by Sergeants Storm and Welsh, the pure knowledge of death serves as final truth or arbiter. In parts inert, quickened in other parts with grisly humor, the novel has the dark density of blood, dividing thinly the mysteries of life and mortality.

Jones is accused of uncouth writing, sensationalism, and naïveté; but though he sometimes gives evidence of these faults, he possesses gifts greater than subtlety: a capacity to respond to life in narrative terms, enduring honesty in statement, a covert uncanny sensitivity. Nor is his achievement limited entirely to war fiction; *Some Came Running* (1957) is set in the small towns of postwar, midwestern America, and *The Merry Month of May* (1971) in Paris during the May riots of 1968.

The Southern Novel

The tradition of Southern fiction is perhaps the oldest in the United States. It goes back to the gothic works of Charles Brockden Brown and Edgar Allan Poe. In the twentieth century, William Faulkner reinvents the South in his myth of Yoknapatawpha County, where history and poetry violently meet. The heroic tradition of Faulkner is fully available to such later writers as Robert Penn Warren, as well as to women novelists who choose to explore more delicate nuances of feeling.

The best of these women novelists—and a figure of "transition" like Warren himself—Eudora Welty (born 1909) captures the concrete quality of life, love, humor, and grotesqueness in her native Mississippi. Her fine stories are collected in *A Curtain of Green* (1941) and *The Wide Net* (1943); and her novels include *Delta Wedding* (1946), *The Golden Apples* (1949), *The Ponder Heart* (1954), and *Losing Battles* (1970). She is adept in rendering, through details of person and place, monstrous or wistful moments that are part of a vanishing Southern existence.

Eudora Welty represents a vanishing way of Southern life. Rural and largely conservative, tragic in its sense of the past, acquainted with bloody defeat and its lingering symbols, struggling still with the guilt of slavery and the stress of industrialization, the South presents a strong regional identity. That identity stands in opposition to the popular assumptions of American culture: progress, egalitarianism, rationalized existence. The Southern mind seems preeminently aware of custom and ceremony, responsive to the mythic or elemental; a mind anxious to preserve the sense of person, family, and community, the folklore of the land; a mind dwelling on the cadences of oral discourse, gossip, rhetoric, and living story. Such is the common image of "Dixie." But novelists—Carson McCullers and Flannery O'Connor, in the postwar years, Faulkner before them—give it darker colorations. They stress alienation, the collapse of values and traditions, the decay of the South. And in the old forms of the gothic and the grotesque, they find new and universal metaphors for man.

The characters of Carson McCullers (1917–1967) are

almost all grotesques, inhabitants of provincial Georgia, left behind on islands of time and their own hermetic souls. For them, the alchemy of love distills only pain. "There are the lover and the beloved," Mrs. McCullers writes, "but these two come from different countries." Without reciprocity, her people diffuse their love, expend it on a hunchback, a rock, a tree, a cloud, and end in greater spiritual solitude. Often maimed or crippled, their bodies mime the distortions of their spirit.

Thus, in her first and longest work, *The Heart is a Lonely Hunter* (1940), a sexless deaf-mute, Singer, serves as mock confessor to a town whose citizens he can neither hear nor heal. Everyone seeks Singer because, as one of the characters puts it, "in some men it is in them to give up everything personal at some time, before it ferments and poisons. . . . The text is 'All men seek for Thee.'" But Singer, who loves another deaf-mute, Antonapoulos, finally commits suicide; the freak as sacrificial hero acts only as ironic Christ, as ambiguous redeemer. Faint echoes of Nazi tyranny in Europe, of the Depression in America, of racial prejudice in the South can be heard in this novel, which remains, more than a social document of the region, a search for communion, a study of immolation.

Next comes *Reflections in a Golden Eye* (1941), set in a military reservation, and *The Member of the Wedding* (1946), a gentle tale of adolescent awakening that is made into a successful play. But the best work of Carson McCullers may be *The Ballad of the Sad Café* (1951), in which Amazon-like Miss Amelia, her hunchback "cousin" Lymon, and her husband-for-a-night, evil Marvin Macy, play out the ballad of loneliness and maimed desire and love condemned to loss, while a chain gang suffers, sings, endures. In the small dreary town, behind shutters, the face of Miss Amelia will still appear, a face "sexless and white, with two gray crossed eyes which are turned inward so sharply that they seem to be exchanging with each other one long secret gaze of grief."

When she is not at her best, as in *Clock Without Hands* (1961), Mrs. McCullers merely speaks for freakish life in tones of pathos. Far more often, however, she writes a tawny prose, rich and yet spare, firm even in its evocations of the most inward self. There, beyond love or pain, her style penetrates the mystery of human sadness.

More precise in embodying mystery through manners, her great rigor equal to her wit and compassion, Flannery O'Connor (1925–1964) is hailed as one of the most impressive postwar writers before her untimely death. In her native Georgia, she sees Protestant fundamentalism run wild, sees worship, heresy, and nihilism within the Bible Belt; and in cities of the North, she sees liberal thought ignore the deeper agonies of humankind. A devout Catholic herself—and a fine essayist on the craft of fiction, whose statements are posthumously collected in *Mystery and Manners* (1969)— she defines her subject as the "action of grace in territory held largely by the devil." The phrase expresses her belief that evil springs wherever the spirit refuses mediation in forms of communal existence or incarnation in gestures of love; the pure gothic impulse, isolation or pride, is invariably demonic.

This belief shapes her first novel, *Wise Blood* (1952), a taut and terrifying tale of a young revivalist preacher converted to the Church Without Christ. "No truth behind all truths is what I and this church preach," Haze Motes cries. In his demented search for godlessness, Haze exposes sins all around him: greed, hypocrisy, indifference—the death of spirit. Even the innocent boy, Enoch Emery, looking for simple human recognition, finding it nowhere, is forced to make some embalmed figure his "jesus," and to don a gorilla suit in order to communicate with his fellow man. Haze blasphemes, rages, mortifies himself; he goes so far as to kill a fake prophet. Thus, negation in his case becomes the voice of twisted divine love. This is also the intuition of Miss O'Connor's second novel, *The Violent Bear It Away* (1960). With steady eye and ruthless humor, she develops in the ritual of baptism a metaphor of the human struggle *against* salvation. Thus, the boy Tarwater holds out fanatically against his fate, until he experiences evil firsthand. Finally, he turns away from pride; his conversion leads him to the fulfillment of his great-uncle's prophecy.

Miss O'Connor also writes extraordinary short stories, *A Good Man Is Hard to Find* (1955) and *Everything That Rises Must Converge* (1965). Complex in comic shadings as in dramatic detail, the stories dwell rather too insistently on horrors that make the human condition intolerable without grace; thus, in a sense, the stories serve less as evidence of our original lapse than as invocations of our redemption. Still, her ascetic control of nuance in the face of baleful passion, her realism in depths and distances, empower her to state the disorders of the contemporary spirit in ineluctable forms, Southern only in texture, universal as death.

Southern fiction, waning somewhat in vitality, continues in still younger writers. But notable as they seem, such novels as William Goyen's *The House of Breath* (1950), Shirley Ann Grau's *The Hard Blue Sky* (1958), Walker Percy's *The Moviegoer* (1961), and Reynolds Price's *A Long and Happy Life* (1962) can not prevent a critical shift of interest to other types of fiction.

The Jewish Novel

The Jewish novel shows no evidence of decline, only of diversity and development into genres as far flung as black humor and historical romance. All Jewish writers, of course, do not concern themselves exclusively with the "Jewish experience." Some, like Mailer, Bellow, or Salinger, accept no restriction on their material; others, like Malamud, writing mainly about Jews, move always into a far broader nexus of life.

Northern in its tradition, urban, liberal or radical in politics, the postwar Jewish novel claims writers as different as Henry Roth, Daniel Fuchs, and Nathanael West as precursors. Through Roth's *Call It Sleep* (1934), Fuchs's *Homage to Blenholt* (1936), and West's *Miss Lonelyhearts* (1933), tragic fact and grotesque feeling, the aches of the ghetto✓ and the anguish of dreams, are made available to the imagination. A more distant influence, Isaac Bashevis Singer recovers from his native Poland a rich Yiddish tradition—*The Family Moskat* (1950), *Satan in Goray* (1955), *The Magician of Lublin* (1960), *The Slave* (1962), *The Manor* (1967)— hedged by his own ironic metaphysic.

Thus, Orthodox Judaism, which rests on a particular faith and history, a sense of community, a language, submits to subtle mutations in postwar America. Memories of the Nazi holocausts and news of Israel's victories concern the Jewish-American novelist who participates in the crucial events of his people only vicariously; even the anti-Semitism he may recall from his own childhood has waned. Anxious and ambivalent, he often expresses the tensions of skepticism and belief, assimilation and identity, new mixed marriages and old family manners, in complex forms. An ancient equilibrist of pain and humor, scapegoat and pariah, he sees in his condition a symbol, not retrograde but prophetic, of the human condition. He creates characters, *schlemiels* or *schlimazels*, of acute sophistication who whisper their infrangible love or innocence.

The premature death of Edward Lewis Wallant (1926–1962) deprives American letters of a novelist of unusual talent and integrity. Though he often writes about Jews, his constant theme—the regeneration of feeling in love or grief, in responsiveness to the sacramental nature of existence—applies to all. His best work, *The Pawnbroker* (1961), follows Sol Nazerman, former victim of Nazi torture, to his rebirth through "agonizing sensitivity" decades after in New York. Wallant's *The Tenants of Moonbloom* (1963) and *The Children at the Gate* (1964), quiet and stringent fictions, confirm his importance posthumously.

Jewish novelists, too many to enumerate, explore various aspects of experience in various ways. Daniel Stern (born 1928), for instance, combines the European experience of concentration camps with that of a Broadway stage production in *Who Shall Live, Who Shall Die* (1963); and writes about the improvised life, urgent and dislocated with hope, in New York in *After the War* (1967). But he is best known for *The Suicide Academy* (1968), which creates a metaphor of the contemporary world, balanced intricately in the dance of affirmation and denial, hovering in the dialogue of Black and Jew. The atmosphere of "para-reality," funny and darkly scintillant, leaves the reader with a brilliant sense of himself. In *The Rose Rabbi* (1971) Stern goes farther in putting the conscience of a Jew on trial, judged not only by the facts of the world but also by Time and Love.

For Bruce Jay Friedman (born 1930), black humor—he even edits an anthology by that name—is the implicit form of skepticism, fear, and the horrors of love. The breakneck gaiety of his novels, *Stern* (1962) and *A Mother's Kisses* (1964), conceals an exacerbated sensitivity to anti-Semitism, to the farce of sex. A social as well as a sexual satirist, Friedman descries all the absurd little amenities and salacities of contemporary life in bright, desperate prose, bright as his own vision is sometimes brittle.

Of the younger Jewish novelists, Philip Roth (born 1933) is the most popular. He first makes an impression with a collection of stories, *Goodbye, Columbus* (1959) which exposes the new Jewish sensibility in a milieu of social and moral ambiguity. Among the stories, "The Conversion of the Jews," "Defender of the Faith," and "Eli, the Fanatic" have become classics in their genre; Roth sees situations clearly, and his style has a kind of creamy humor. His two subsequent works, the novels *Letting Go* (1962) and *When She Was Good* (1967)—the latter shows no concern whatever with Jewish matters—deal with sex, ambition, responsibility, the savage boredom and banality of culture. Impressive in dialogue and dramatic action, these novels are nevertheless fairly conventional. With *Portnoy's Complaint* (1969), however, Roth creates a pleasant scandal. Focusing on a Jewish family, and particularly on the relation between possessive mother and prodigal son, Roth writes a ribald fantasy of guilt and onanism, altruism and prurience. The humor of the tale catches the current erotic mood of fiction and deflects violence toward insight. The sexual conflict between Gentile and Jew in his earlier stories here moves to a deeper level, involving self-knowledge and self-fantasy. Still, despite his great skill and hilarity, Roth does not always guard himself against a certain triviality.

Other authors, such as Herbert Gold, Stanley Elkin, Grace Paley, Herbert Wilner, and Wallace Markfield, prove that the Jewish novel draws on a wide range of talent and continues to present the manners, humors, and meditations of a central region of the postwar world.

The Black Novel

The character of Black fiction changes rapidly as the Afro-American community develops a new cultural and political sense of itself. Nevertheless, certain outlines of the novel emerge since Richard Wright (1908–1960) gives it shape with *Uncle Tom's Children* (1938), *Native Son* (1940), and *Black Boy* (1945). Memories of slavery, protest and fury,

the contradictory search for dignity in a world dominated
by white values, the conflict between the artistic and political natures of the writer, his sexual complexities, the existential quality of his life, his need for an ethnic definition
of himself—all these appear, sometimes in hints, sometimes
fully developed, in Wright's work. Wright says: "The Negro
is America's metaphor." The Negro may also be an image
of man under certain conditions of urgency or stress, deriving life from an inner source as Mailer and Kerouac come
to see, an outsider who nonetheless engages the guilt, fantasy, and violence of others, and thus embodies an historic
revelation.

These are precisely the challenges that Ralph Ellison
(born 1914) meets in his outstanding novel, *Invisible Man*
(1952). Born in Oklahoma, Ellison does not feel all the
restraints that the old slave states impose on their Blacks;
his sense of the human condition therefore tends to be more
complex, more expansive than some Black militants allow.
In his collection of essays, *Shadow and Act* (1964), he states:
"You know, the skins of those thin-legged little girls who
faced the mob in Little Rock marked them as Negro but the
spirit which directed their feet is the old universal urge
toward freedom." A born artist, educated in sculpture and
music, he shows a sophisticated sense of forms, the "mixture
of the marvelous and the terrible," as well as a sense of jazz-
like improvisation. He learns from his own experience as
much as from the blues how anger, incongruity, and agony
can sustain a provisional vision of things.

The task of that ironic picaresque, the nameless hero of
Invisible Man, is exactly this: to move from invisibility to
vision. Through the dangers, corruptions, and temptations
awaiting him, he recapitulates the history of his own race,
conducting a ceaseless "psychological scrimmage" with everyone, himself included. Exploited by all—white Communists
and African nationalists, Southern bigots and Northern lib-

erals, women and men alike—he proceeds, less in the manner of an arrow than a boomerang, from innocence to disillusionment to the edge of a new wisdom, a dialectic sense of himself. In the surreal cool cellar lit by 1,369 light bulbs where he ends, he perceives the essential chaos of the mind, and finds freedom in a form that can "condemn and affirm, say no and say yes, say yes and say no." *Invisible Man* is a profound and brilliant work, which engages issues of History, Soul, and Art still alive in our midst. It may be criticized for being too prolix, too diffuse, in specific parts; yet the novel is resourceful in its syncopation of reality, musical in its organization of themes, its screams and grotesque laughter issuing from a heroic consciousness willing to surrender nothing to its own ease. Ellison's novel is more than an example of Black fiction; it stands as an early landmark in all of postwar literature.

James Baldwin (born 1924) makes his impact in more diverse ways: in fiction, in drama, above all in essays at once lucid and impassioned, burning with self-knowledge. His statements in *Notes of a Native Son* (1955), *Nobody Knows My Name* (1961), and *The Fire Next Time* (1963) sound a crescendo of anger that echoes his own growing perplexity in relation to even more militant Blacks. Ellison's Invisible Man asks: "Who knows but that, on the lower frequencies, I speak for you?" This, too, is Baldwin's belief, though the temptations of rancor and rage seem to him more harrowing; a cloud always stands between Black men and the sun. Self-exiled in Paris for a decade, 1948–58, he returns to America, knowing that his European stay can only be a preparation for that terrible journey back. Since then, Baldwin has served as a spokesman for the artistic conscience in its struggle with its Black inheritance, in its aspiration to a human estate.

His first novel, the autobiographical *Go Tell It On The Mountain* (1953), depicts the family of a Harlem preacher, a proud, lust-driven man haunted by the power of a terrible God. Religion howls in poetry; prophecy, sin, and madness shake the soul of young Johnny, bastard stepson of the family, who makes his way through torment to manhood. Flawed and still impressive, the book promises great fictional talent, which Baldwin has not yet realized. In two subsequent novels, *Another Country* (1962) and *Tell Me How Long the Train's Been Gone* (1968), he attempts to place racial and political conflicts in an erotic focus. His intricate and sinuous style, graceful or apocalytic as the occasion requires, is unmistakable; but his materials seem to defy dramatic control. The Black race and the White, straight and inverted sex, worldly and transcendent concerns, often break asunder in rhetoric, fury, or sentiment.

The difficulties of any writer in a revolutionary movement can be immense; it is therefore all the more remarkable that Black authors, who do not always agree on a common stance, manage still to fulfill themselves in literature. Some, like William Demby (born 1926) choose exile. Writing in Rome, he finds the international modernist style most congenial to him. His first novel, *Beetlecreek* (1950), expresses his revulsion, his disaffiliation; but in *The Catacombs* (1965), a learned novel of the space age, a cubist fiction and intellectual pastiche of history, Demby succeeds in giving his reconciliation a universal form. Others, writing in the shadow of Wright, Ellison, and Baldwin, find their own voice in the Sixties. John A. Williams (born 1925), active in many political and literary endeavors, moved deeply by Black anger, committed still to art, produces fine, laconic novels in *Sissie* (1963) and *The Man Who Cried I Am* (1967). Paule Marshall (born 1929), born in Brooklyn of Barbadian parents, draws on her knowledge of South, Central, and North America in *Brown Girl, Brownstone* (1959) and *Soul Clap Hands and Sing* (1961). The recipient of numerous literary awards, William Melvin Kelley (born 1937) proves his undeniable talent in *A Different Drummer* (1962) and *Dem* (1967). *A Different Drummer*, blending narrative and legend with some Faulknerian overtones, relates the strange flight of Tucker Caliban and the entire Black population of a Southern state, seen from the point of view of various characters; and *Dem*, maintaining uneasy control of its greater anger, describes the mores, the psychic life, of Northern Whites from a Black vantage, taking its theme from the Ashanti proverb: "The ruin of a nation begins in the homes. of its people."

Clearly, Black fiction, which remained for several decades in the custody of a few authors, promises great power and diversity in years to come, as the works of Julian Mayfield, Ronald Fair, Cecil Brown, Chester Himes, and Ishmael Reed show.

Alienation and Anarchy

By far the largest part of contemporary literature comes under the rubric of alienation—alienation certainly from the dominant culture, alienation sometimes from self and nature. The fictional hero is an outsider because the very conditions of life, of his own consciousness, require estrangement. The forms of estrangement, however, evolve curiously in the postwar years.

Paul Bowles (born 1910) is among the earliest writers to turn his back on American, indeed, on Western culture. The characters of his novels, *The Sheltering Sky* (1949) and *Let It Come Down* (1953), are expatriates in a stark and pitiless land, North Africa; and their existential quest, which recalls Camus's *The Stranger*, ends in annihilation. His stories in *The Delicate Prey* (1950) contrast the worlds of nature and civilization, instinct and reason, exposing unfit Americans to extreme situations: murder, suicide, rape, incest, drugs, torture, madness. The sinister transformation of Bowles's heroes from pilgrims into prey parallels the self-destructive impulse of the West; his work presages, in a style of classic restraint, the wandering Beats, and, more precisely, the violent Hipsters.

The Beat Movement, of course, has a sacramental aspect lacking in Bowles's world. The Beats invoke Christ and Buddha, Thoreau and Whitman, the mystic plenitude of America, in the very act of denying its flaccid culture. Emerging from the coffee houses of San Francisco, Venice West, or Greenwich Village, these new bohemians spread across the land, challenging the forms and values of middle-class culture, devising a shaggy life style of their own, which features sex, drugs, jazz, material simplicity. Love and anarchy jostle in the movement, as Jack Kerouac (1922–1969) best exemplifies. His novel *On the Road* (1957) · attempts to recover the spontaneity of jazz, the perception of *haiku*, the wildness and openness and joy of the American continent. Its hero, Dean Moriarty, a drop-out from civilization, "holy goof," intones: "What's your road, man?—holy boy road, madman road, rainbow road, guppy road, any road." Kerouac's next novel, *The Subterraneans* (1958), is a love idyll of the underground, sung in sweet "spontaneous prose," loosened in syntax, flowing with the natural line of feeling. But his best work may be *The Dharma Bums* (1958), which celebrates the "rucksack revolution," the splendors of Eastern religion and of the American West, the cities with their gritty loves in the background, the very wonder of creation. Though Kerouac can be maudlin and slapdash, and his imagination limited by its Beat mystique, he sees both the sadness and energy of ragged America, and its holy terror.

The Beat mystique can be traced in some other novels, both earlier and later than Kerouac's: R. V. Cassill's *The Eagle on the Coin* (1950), John Clellon Holmes's *Go* (1952), Chandler Brossard's *Who Walk in Darkness* (1952), Norman

Mailer's *The Deer Park* (1955), Lawrence Ferlinghetti's *Her* (1960), Alexander Trocchi's *Cain's Book* (1960), and Jack Gelber's *On Ice* (1964). But as many of these novels suggest, another attitude begins to emerge from Beat literature: more hardened or dangerous, familiar with crime, drugs, perversion, acquainted with nihilism in the bone, the night of the Hipster.

The Hipster goes farther in metaphysical rebellion, and none goes farther in his fictional exploration of that state than William Burroughs (born 1914). Indeed, Burroughs defines a limit beyond which neither language nor form can go in the American novel. The violence of his work is cold and total: junk, violent homosexuality, totalitarianism provide him merely with obscene metaphors for a spent universe, ruled by entropy, moving toward apocalypse. Unlike the Beats, whom he favors from a distance, Burroughs has no romantic exuberance in him; yet his style, mechanical and desiccated, can still break into outrageous humor and poetic hallucination. In his best work, *Naked Lunch* (1959), he offers a lunatic film scenario, a grisly montage of satire and horror —reminiscent in parts of Hieronymus Bosch—showing humanity in the demonic control of abstract powers, powers working through sex, through drugs, through language itself, to reduce life to death and excrement. An experimentalist in the American vein of anti-literature, Burroughs finds words abysmally corrupt: "To speak is to lie," he says. In the technological nightmares of his later "science fiction" (which I discuss under that heading), he turns to "The Cut-Up Method," which demands composition by random collages of clippings.

Other novels express alienation in terms of violence and perversion so shocking as to approach Burroughs's: John Rechy's *City of Night* (1963), Burt Blechman's *Stations* (1964), Hubert Selby's *Last Exit to Brooklyn* (1964). (The theme of murderous homosexuality goes back to Gore Vidal's

The City and the Pillar [1948].) But none of these exceeds the satanic wit and distrust of language in Burroughs's work. Alienation and anarchy revert, thereafter, to a very different attitude, to new antics of an archaic figure: the amorous rogue, master of chicaneries.

Such is Sebastian Dangerfield, hero of J. P. Donleavy's (born 1926) *The Ginger Man* (1955, 1958, 1965). Scruffy, zany sensualist, he lurches through Dublin, improvising his life from day to day with all the gusto and desperation he can muster. But the comic vitality of the novel, which ridicules mediocrity and convention, also has a nasty edge; it is sharpened on death. This salacious picaresque, banned at first in several countries, becomes a prototype of quest and skullduggery, man determined to be himself outside of all restraints, and to evade absurd mortality. Written in an original, elliptic style, interspersed with bitter twaddling songs, *The Ginger Man* offers a vision of human singularity under the aspect of desperate laughter. Donleavy's subsequent works, such as *A Singular Man* (1963) and *The Beastly Beatitudes of Balthazar B* (1968), are sad, shy, lewd, hilarious, and death-haunted, but do not alter that vision.

The novel of alienation reaches the limits of outrage in *Naked Lunch*, and prompts the bitter tomfooleries of *The Ginger Man*. But it also generates, in such works as the *The Dharma Bums*, a redemptive impulse beyond alienation. This is clear in the work of Ken Kesey (born 1935). His extraordinary first novel, *One Flew Over the Cuckoo's Nest* (1962), set in a mental institution, shows how the unbroken spirit of one man, McMurphy, an outsider to the deadly "combine" of social existence, which Big Nurse personifies, can free his fellow inmates, free them even from their own fear before life. Significantly, it is an Indian, Big Chief, who recovers that freedom. Kesey's second novel, *Sometimes a Great Notion* (1964), attracts less attention than a journalistic account, Tom Wolfe's *The Electric Kool-Aid Acid Test* (1968), of Kesey's zany, psychedelic years as head Merry Prankster.

Yet the redemptive impulse, the movement out of alienation, seems more cruel in the work of Jerzy Kosinski (born
1933). Born in Poland, Kosinski draws on European as well
as American conditions of solitude. His shattering first novel,
The Painted Bird (1966), depicts with preternatural clarity
the tortures and savageries that a boy, taken for a Gypsy
or Jew, tries to escape in Nazi-occupied Poland. *Steps* (1968)
pursues through lacunae of the unspeakable the adventures
of a young man in America. The hero, forced by memory
and circumstance to act as predator, is also a symbol of the
contemporary Self, pure in its extreme self-consciousness,
struggling to reenter the world with the lucidity of hatred.
Spare in style, learned in the dark nuances of the human,
consummately parabolic, Kosinski transcends the platitudes
of alienation. A third novel, *Being There* (1971) leads him
to explore some comic equivalents of that theme and to
redefine the social clichés of estrangement.

Thus, the fiction of estrangement implies heroism as well
as terror and comedy in America.

From Satire to the Novel of the Absurd

One of the more recent and salient trends of postwar fiction
is a variant of fantasy, satirical only in part, inward with
absurdity. Both celebration and despondency mingle in its
motive, though its humor tends to be Stygian. The authors
drawn to the genre display great inventiveness, verbal magic
and virtuosity, versatility even in despair. Their parodies do
not reflect only upon the distempers of society and the foibles
of man; they reflect, more fundamentally, on the failures of
history or art, the radical disease of consciousness itself.

The line from Nathanael West and Vladimir Nabokov to
John Barth, Joseph Heller, Thomas Berger, Thomas Pynchon,

Terry Southern, and Donald Barthelme is not as straight as critics might wish. The line, quite real in its dark comic fiber, also loops in many stray strands.

In a special sense, the satirical work of Mary McCarthy (born 1912), though conventional, may be rather apposite to the new spirit of comedy. Her acidulous observations of Leftist intellectuals in *The Oasis* (1949), of collegiate intriguers in *The Groves of Academe* (1952), of art colonists and bohemians in *A Charmed Life* (1955), of women and wives, lesbians and big-city careerists in *The Group* (1963) convey a cold intuition of American life and manners. From her vantage point abroad—she makes her home in Paris— she perceives swift humor and horror in contemporary society but disguises from herself a deeper distaste of existence.

A satirist of more benign disposition, John Cheever (born 1912) approaches American experience with a genuine narrative gift and a sacramental wink at life. He maps out, he creates, a cultural milieu of upper middle-class exurbanites with uncanny humor, and sees people with eccentric clarity. His cunning stories, collected in *The Way Some People Live* (1943), *The Enormous Radio* (1953), *The Housebreaker of Shady Hill* (1958), wryly reveal the small, daily miracles or damnations of existence. Love and celebration, whimsy and irony, render his history of a New England family, in *The Wapshot Chronicle* (1957) and *The Wapshot Scandal* (1964), into a testimony not only American in its generosities but also human in its dalliance with fate. Despite his eroticism and exuberance, though, Cheever also knows the "nightmare of our existence" and states: "Life in the United States in 1960 is Hell." This intuition sometimes expresses itself too coyly in his fiction; his Gehennas appear too glossy.

The contemporary Hell appears as organized chaos to the absurdist sensibility, a kind of institutionalized madness. This is how the world appears to Joseph Heller (born 1923), who writes in *Catch-22* (1961) a masterpiece of black comedy. Ostensibly a "war novel," dealing with the attempts of Air Force Captain Yossarian to stay alive and sane through bombing missions without end, the book creates a surreal universe of drollery and death. The universe of death, "boiling in chaos in which everything was in proper order," includes private as well as public motives, includes sex, money, and war; and it obeys only the demented logic of "catch number 22," the gratuitous defeat of man. Serious, satirical, and unspeakably funny, the novel bursts in fragments of dialogue, narrative, caricature, joke, reflection, flashback. Its worlds of reference within reference—militarism, bureaucracy, America, the modern world, the human condition—collide in a disorder that only Heller's imagination can contain, only his discontinuous form can render with integrity.

Conscience modifies the sense of incongruity in another novelist too sophisticated for piety, too vigorous for despair—Thomas Berger (born 1924). His style, extravagant, buffoonish, recovers for man a kind of quixotic innocence or simplicity. Like the hero of his Reinhart novels, *Crazy in Berlin* (1958), *Reinhart in Love* (1962), *Vital Parts* (1970), Berger impersonates the Fool or Scapegoat of tradition, carrier away of death, and makes his home in the fictive and real worlds with equal poise. His method depends upon a sustained tension between meaning and absurdity, desire and death, a jocular sciomachy that Reinhart sustains at various stages of his life. Berger writes big books lavishly—*Little Big Man* (1964), spoofing the western, *Killing Time* (1967), spoofing the mystery—losing himself in slapstick sometimes, also discovering strange philosophies of the heart. In his world of implausibility, serious things are seldom certain or absolute.

In the world of Terry Southern (born 1928) satire and black humor, parody and pornography, tend toward Camp. But his best work, *Flash and Filigree* (1958) or *The Magic Christian* (1960), is also pitiless in its contempt for human deceit and folly. A master of the lingos of the underground as well as of mass media, Southern shows his versatility by contributing to erotica in *Candy* (1964), and to the filmscript of Stanley Kubrick's *Dr. Strangelove.*

A more serious humorist, a creative fantastick, Donald Barthelme (born 1931) experiments with non-linear narratives and absurdist techniques—his works include fragments, pictures, questionnaires, catalogues, collages, captions of various size—while maintaining his commitment to a world wildly out of joint. His novel *Snow White* (1967), his stories in *Unspeakable Practices, Unnatural Acts* (1968) or in *City Life* (1970), show fierce wit and verbal agility as well as a genuine, if totally oblique, moral perception of our collective lunacy. In these fictions, human experience repels value judgments; we learn the phenomenology of a trite existence, its sludge and trash. Mockingly, Barthelme asks: "Do you feel that the creation of new modes of hysteria is a viable undertaking for the artist of today? Yes ( ) No ( )." His own work provides more than one playful answer.

But none pushes the absurd novel farther toward autodestruction and pessimistic play than Thomas Pynchon (born 1937). Arcane humor, bizarre characters, cryptic plots and counterplots, a style almost too brilliant in puns, allusions, innuendos, all serve his purpose: the obliteration of meaning, the revelation of secret yet continuous decay in life *and* of the patterns that inhere even in decay. His first novel, *V* (1963), designs a labyrinthine story of mock quests leading nowhere—except, perhaps, to the destructive center of the twentieth century. History and consciousness, love and identity, science and art, language and silence, form a fantastic game, part nonsense and part indeterminacy, whose rules are written in the void. (The author seems like one of his characters, a painter drawing a picture on the hull of a sinking ship in mid-ocean!) In *The Crying of Lot 49* (1966), Pynchon continues his inspired reduction of the world's absurdity with lyric and mock-apocalyptic fervor. As in his previous work, sex, violence, madness, and technology compose an entropic hallucination of the void, an epistemological conundrum. Thus the heroine of the book, Oedipa Maas, becomes the cryptologist of an occult America, and of a hermetic system of pervasive yet silent communication called The Tristero. In the process, her vision calls itself into question just as the involutions of her author's imagination cast doubt on everything. An exotic Joycean, Pynchon seems at times less paranoiac than precious, a Camp anti-novelist, insidious in his knowledge of icy sadness, the pathos of waste.

Science Fiction

Fantasy may also take the special form of science fiction, which gains increasingly in prestige as well as popularity. Long held in dubiety, the genre finds in the climate of the postwar age—beginning with atomic explosions, continuing with explorations of space and moon landings—much to give it new authority. Science fiction provides a myth of technological man, citizen of an expanding universe. Through its forms, both the creative and destructive potentials of current experience can be made visible; and the imagination finds a way of confronting stunning changes in culture or consciousness. Oriented toward the future, it criticizes the present; anticipating the apocalypse, it urges perfection. Thus, science fiction tends to be prophetic, visionary in its invocations of utopia, as well as satirical, minatory in its projections of dystopia. Beneath its peculiar mythopoetics of hope lurks some violent unease, expressing, more than a fear of dehumanization, man's terror of the void, annihilation of his selfhood.

Many writers better known for other kinds of fiction turn

to science fiction. William Burroughs, for instance, turns in his more recent work—*The Soft Machine* (1961, 1965), *The Ticket that Exploded* (1962, 1967), and *Nova Express* (1964)—to an intergalactic adventure and moral drama involving the conflict between forces of good and evil, freedom and repression, couched in a technological language, simulating a space-age nightmare. Burroughs himself prefers to see his fantasy as a new mythology for our time, replacing old decrepit forms. "Love plays little part in my mythology . . ." he says, and "none of the characters . . . are free."

Kurt Vonnegut also finds science fiction congenial, albeit in a very different mood. One of his fictional characters, Eliot Rosewater, cries: "You're [science fiction writers] all I read any more. You're the only ones who'll talk about the *really* terrific changes going on, the only ones crazy enough to know that life is a space voyage. . . . " Vonnegut's own novels, such as *The Sirens of Titan* (1959) and *Cat's Cradle* (1963), employing the techniques of science fiction both in a satirical and visionary vein, become the center of an intense cult among American youths.

The genre also develops in various and ingenious ways among professional science fiction authors. Some of these begin by publishing early in the two space-blazing magazines, Hugo Gernsback's *Amazing Stories*, started in 1926, and John W. Campbell's *Astounding Stories*, founded in 1938; others come on the scene later, in the early Fifties, writing for Horace L. Gold's *Galaxy Science Fiction*, which insists on philosophic seriousness as well as scientific plausibility. It becomes clear that the old space thrillers—*Buck Rogers, Flash Gordon, Superman*—no longer exhaust the genre.

Though science fiction writers are too numerous and prolific to treat adequately here, at least four of them should be cited. Robert Heinlein (born 1907), among the oldest and most accomplished, is known best for *Stranger in a Strange Land* (1961), which engages the social and religious aspirations of the counter-culture, but also inspires the demonic commune of Charles Manson. Heinlein's books, which include *The Man Who Sold the Moon* (1950), *Starship Troopers* (1959), and *Glory Road* (1963), tend to affirm the possibilities of man in the universe. Less voluminous, Alfred Bester (born 1913) gives us, in *The Demolished Man* (1953), a fine example of how science fiction can envisage expansions in human awareness, alternatives to the present. *The Stars My Destination* (1957) and *Starburst* (1958) also reveal his imaginative possession of the form. Drawing on his boundless expertise and energy, Isaac Asimov (born 1920) formulates, in such works as *Pebble in the Sky* (1950), *Foundation* (1951), *The Currents of Space* (1952), *The End of Eternity* (1955), his concern for the impact of science on human affairs. More precisely, he defines the genre as "that branch of literature which deals with a fictitious society, differing from our own chiefly in the nature or extent of its technological development." Perhaps more poetic than any writer in this group, Ray Bradbury (born 1920), who does not limit himself to science fiction, also shows a vivid gift of characterization and a mastery of illusionism in such books as *The Martian Chronicles* (1950), *The Illustrated Man* (1951), *Fahrenheit 451* (1953), *R is for Rocket* (1962), *S is for Space* (1966). Behind the illusionism loom significant cultural realities of our time.

Science fiction can be philosophically naïve, morally simple, aesthetically willed or crude. Yet, at its best, it seems to touch a nerve of the collective dream, to release some fantasy locked within our machines. At its best, it can enlarge the realm of human possibilities.

III

POETRY

INTRODUCTION

Postwar American verse is both abundant and contrary. Styles break out, changing rapidly; cliques form and disappear; poets proliferate. Now confusion, now controversy reign. At times, it seems as if nothing very great is at stake. Certainly no poet, except Lowell or Ginsberg, projects the charisma of laureates or *poètes maudits* of another age. In 1961 Lowell says: "It's quite hard to think of a young poet who has the validity of Salinger or Saul Bellow." Since then, of course, Salinger recedes into silence, and Lowell himself becomes a literary eminence. Yet his statement catches the constraint of the new poetry, its perversity. Poets of quality are no fewer than novelists; they publish, teach, read more widely than ever before; fellowships come their way, and small magazines honor their work; translators render them into foreign tongues. Various academic presses also sponsor their work in such projects as the Wesleyan Poetry Program, the Pitt Poetry Series, and the Contemporary Poets Series of the University of North Carolina, all in paperback, and the Yale Series of Younger Poets in hardback. Yet poets also pay a heavy psychic toll to Mammon, in suicide, madness, mute despair; and in the end, their impact on the age seems less than they deserve.

It is otherwise with the generation of modernists in whose shadow the postwar poets begin to write; the influence of the former prolongs the apprenticeship of the latter, eases them into orthodoxy. Literary historians consistently argue that the first breakthrough of the century comes when Pound and Eliot, writing in London, turn to French Symbolism, English Metaphysical verse, or ancient Provençal lyrics to fashion a language that brings Victorian or Georgian modes to an end. This language is formal, erudite, compressed in thought, elusive in rhythms, quick to the uses of irony and wit, rich in conceits or catachresis, inclined to mythical allusions. The difficult and original effort of Pound and Eliot soon establishes a movement, enriched by the work of Conrad Aiken, Wallace Stevens, and Hart Crane. The New Critics, who include such notable poets as John Crowe Ransom and Allen Tate, lend their intellectual authority to this movement. Editors and academics, through critical quarterlies, through college courses, support its orthodoxies. Despite the divergent influence of Auden in the Thirties, the tradition still imposes near the end of World War II "restrictions of a benevolent tyranny." These words of a younger poet, Donald Hall, describe the onus that some of his elders—Stanley Kunitz, Richard Eberhart, Theodore Roethke, Elizabeth Bishop, Randall Jarrell, Karl Shapiro, Robert Lowell, Richard Wilbur—probably feel during the Forties.

When the reaction to orthodoxy finally comes, it takes a multitude of forms; and some postwar poets who begin in one manner shift dramatically to another. Different models, as indigenous as Walt Whitman, Carl Sandburg, or Robert Frost, are rediscovered. Instead of the decorous and polyglot cadences of the modernist tradition, the raucous sounds of American speech come into verse. Curiously enough, an aspect of the later Pound—idiomatic, immediate, discontinuous as the *Cantos*—is recovered together with the poetry of William Carlos Williams, who provides an informal paradigm, the accents and diction of urban life, a poetry of experience. The rebellious romanticism of E. E. Cummings and the mystic tone of H. D. seem also apposite. Elegance, polish, precision, give way to assertions both more intensely personal and publicly more vociferous. The earlier tradition of Eliot, which becomes academic, yields to new styles of confession or protest, surrealism or bardic rage, claiming the ancestry of Whitman. Spiritually, these styles look toward the Pacific not Europe, look to nature rather than culture. Certain schools or coteries begin to acquire a name: the Black Mountain poets (Charles Olson, Robert Creeley); the Beats (Allen Ginsberg, Gregory Corso); the San Francisco poets (Robert Duncan, Lawrence Ferlinghetti); the New York poets (John Ashbery, Kenneth Koch); the Neo-Romantics (W. D. Snodgrass, Robert Bly). Many other poets, vaguely anti-formalist, fall in no category. The audiences of all these writers tend to be younger, more radical in politics, experimental in their cultural styles.

Discriminations between these two main trends of postwar poetry are at best tentative, at worst misleading. Yet certain terms come into use, sharpening both contrast and controversy. Lowell casually distinguishes between "cooked" and "raw" verse, and Ferlinghetti between poetry of "the ivory tower" and poetry of "the streets." Others pit "academic" against "beat." In some sense, these labels revert to the old strains in American literature, which Philip Rahv calls "pale face" (Poe, James) and "red skin" (Melville, Twain); revert, indeed, to Nietzsche's fundamental distinction between the

"Apollonian" and "Dionysian" temperaments. Perhaps we can simply refer to the older modernist style as "closed," the newer as "open," keeping in mind that boundaries are never so clear as to warrant a last judgment, that most poets progress in their individual careers from the former to the latter. Commenting on a generation of poets of which he is himself a member, Daniel Hoffman puts it simply: "Different as these poets are from one another, each has passed in his own way through a similar progress: early mastery of received modes and forms, the intensification of these traditional materials, then the struggle to free the tongue from accustomed language, the ear from familiar cadences, the eye from habitual ways of seeing, the sensibility from conventional responses to experience."

The course of postwar poets may follow a certain pattern; but the appearance of the poets themselves in the public domain, the making and fading of their reputations, seems more erratic. These mutations of taste are reflected in leading anthologies of the period. Thus, Louis Untermeyer's early selection, *Modern American Poetry* (1950), includes Kenneth Patchen, Elizabeth Bishop, Delmore Schwartz, Muriel Rukeyser, Karl Shapiro, John Berryman, Randall Jarrell, Peter Viereck, and Robert Lowell among poets born after 1910. A revised edition of the same anthology (1962), lists new names: Stanley Kunitz, Barbara Howes, William Jay Smith, W. D. Snodgrass. John Ciardi's *Mid-Century American Poets* (1950), introduces Richard Eberhart, Theodore Roethke, and Richard Wilbur. Oscar Williams's *The New Pocket Anthology of American Verse* (1955) samples Isabella Gardner, Howard Nemerov, Howard Moss, Anthony Hecht, Daniel G. Hoffman, W. S. Merwin, among others. Three poets, Donald Hall, Robert Pack, and Louis Simpson, in *The New Poets of England and America* (1957, 1962), emphasize other poets, such as John Hollander, Donald Justice, William Meredith, May Swenson, James Merrill, Reed Whittermore, Louis Simpson, as well as James Dickey, James Wright, Galway Kinnell, X. J. Kennedy, John Logan, and Denise Levertov, who soon move into less "academic" directions. Against the predominantly closed style of these authors—closed *up to that time*—Donald M. Allen edits his anthology, *The New American Poetry: 1945–1960* (1960), which comprises poets working in a variety of open styles: Charles Olson, Brother Antoninus, Robert Duncan, Denise Levertov, Robert Creeley, Allen Ginsberg, Gary Snyder, Frank O'Hara, John Ashbery. The opposition of these styles is acknowledged in a work edited by Paris Leary and Robert Kelly, called *A Controversy of Poets* (1965). Later anthologies, such as Mark Strand's *The Contemporary American Poets* (1969), draw freely on all manner of poets without allegiance to older distinctions of style or school; and Richard Kostelanetz's *Possibilities of Poetry* (1970) is even more eclectic. With Paul Carroll's *The Young American Poets* (1968) and Geoff Hewitt's *Quickly Aging Here* (1969), entirely new names, projected as poets for the Seventies, begin to appear.

The path through the proverbial wood of contemporary verse is cleared by four poets who begin to publish before the war yet remain very much part of the postwar scene. These authors of transition also exemplify, each in his manner, some tendency of the period.

Richard Eberhart (born 1904) brings to his earliest verse, *A Bravery of Earth* (1930) and *Reading the Spirit* (1937), a breathless romantic intensity, a lyric presence often awkward or naïve, yet, in its vitalist rush, in its intuition of death, immemorially wise. Three decades later, he expresses in *Collected Poems* (1960) other moods: visionary, reflective, didactic, erotic. Conscious always of the insufficiency of art, of the abuses of "modern warring maniacal man," he searches through the soul of the times and his own for the "gift of the true."

Less prolific, a superb craftsman working for many years

without acclaim, Stanley Kunitz (born 1905) publishes *Intellectual Things* (1930) and *Passport to the War* (1944). But it is only with *Selected Poems—1928–1958* (1958), hailed by Lowell among others, that Kunitz is recognized for his precise language, dense yet also natural, metaphysical and unassuming. Stoic, skeptical, he asserts no more than his sudden images or quiet rhythms know, suffering all the while the history of our century, "that wide and mortal pang." The closed style of his earlier work relaxes, turns outward, becomes almost trustful with age, in *The Testing Tree* (1971).

Accomplished in poetry as he is in fiction or criticism, Robert Penn Warren (born 1905) is part of that Southern movement called the Fugitives, led by Ransom and Tate, conservative in cultural outlook, formalist in literature. Power and intelligence inform his verse, and a ballad naïveté toughens its texture. From *Thirty-six Poems* (1936) to the long narrative work *Brother to Dragons* (1953), Warren moves between rhetoric and love. Through an anthology he edits with Cleanth Brooks, *Understanding Poetry* (1938), he influences the first decade of postwar writing with precepts of the New Criticism.

Quite the opposite from Warren, Kenneth Rexroth (born 1905) espouses the cause of various anti-formalists, the San Francisco poets, the Beats. An iconoclast by temper, erudite, crotchety, and generous, his intellectual passions include translations from the Greek, Japanese, Chinese, and essays both literary and polemic. His verses, from *In What Hour* (1940), through *The Collected Shorter Poems* (1966) and *The Collected Longer Poems* (1968), display a curious mixture of Oriental imagism and anarchic fervor in forms stark and free.

The romantic primitivism of Eberhart, the close modulations of language of Kunitz, the complex of irony and earthiness of Warren, and the rebellious prosody of nature of

Rexroth all find their way into contemporary poetry. It remains for younger poets to reconcile the richness of their legacy to huge violence within their lives and without. Ravaged in their sensibility, sometimes to the point of derangement, they break into a post-humanist age.

A MAJOR POET:
ROBERT LOWELL

The stature of Robert Lowell (born 1917) grows continuously over the years, exerting the authority of a major figure. Scion of literary Brahmins—he counts James Russell Lowell and Amy Lowell among his relations—a Nonconformist converted to Catholicism, a conscientious objector imprisoned during the war, later a pacifist active in demonstrations against Vietnam, conservative at the same time in his attitudes toward history, revered by the Southern formalists among whom he counts many friends and esteemed by the powerful New York establishment, his verse taught and dissected by professors of English across the country, Lowell holds a special position of influence. But it is his poetry, of course, that commands respect by its manifest excellence; the original developments of his language set an example of dangerous achievement, almost impossible to emulate.

From the start, Lowell struggles with his daimon. The inheritance of Lowells and of Winslows on the mother's side, the inhibition of his own violence, the sad or sudden paralysis of self, give his poetry its peculiar power. Against inner torment—in some deep, distasteful sympathy with Milton's Satan, Lowell also cries, "I myself am hell"—he pits the disintegration of the world without; and finds in madness a state that can subsume all hells. A central voice, apocalyptic and anecdotal, putting contemporary existence on trial, is heard in unmistakable cadences throughout the phases of his poetry.

The descendant of Puritans, wracked by rebellious guilt, bent under history and bending it back upon itself, Lowell finds in Catholicism the lines of his own spiritual force. His first volume, *Land of Unlikeness* (1944), influenced by Tate and Ransom and by English Metaphysical verse, gives its best pieces to a stronger second volume, *Lord Weary's Castle* (1946). In both, Lowell reveals his dark apprehension of Christ, who contains hope of Redemption for all things dead or dying, "lust and dust." The very structures of the poems imitate the movements of Grace. Their references reach for the American as well as the European past. Their characteristic language is thick, alliterative, gnarled by its kinesthetic metaphors, its conceits working dialectically, the syntax elliptic, the rhythms nearly obsessive—in short, a triumph of the closed style, clotted, Hopkinsian, at times grotesque. Some of Lowell's best poems and his most savage come from these early books, Charon-rowed across some private Styx.

The Mills of the Kavanaughs (1951) offers seven dramatic monologues. The title poem, uncommonly uneven and long, develops reveries, memories, thoughts of a young woman whose husband, a naval officer, has committed suicide. Mythic allusions, particularly to Pluto and Persephone, guide the obscure narrative toward a recognition of Death, "who takes the world on trust." The decline of New England is implicit. Some shorter pieces, notably "Falling Asleep Over the Aeneid" and "Mother Marie Therese," seem better realized. But the interest of the volume is prefigurative; it suggests a shift toward a more easeful dramatic manner.

Life Studies (1960) brings the stunning shift to light. Almost prosaic in parts, strong and yet endlessly subtle in sounds, philosophic without vehemence, elegiac and confessional without laxity, the poems probe past and present, self and civilization, family and friends; "Skunk Hour," "Man and

Wife," "Memories of West Street and Lepke," "Ford Maddox Ford," stand among the best. Lowell speaks through these pieces clearly in his own voice, his Catholic insistencies muted, the great lunacy of existence still there, calm as befits "the tranquillized Fifties." But autobiography—explicit in the marvelous "My Last Afternoon with Uncle Devereux Winslow" and the prose sketch "91 Revere Street"—serves as the form of anguish or vulnerability by which the poet can engage the world. Mischief and satire, a kind of new-found slyness, appear; ironical, Lowell wants to undercut nostalgia as well as pain. He can write masterfully, in "Waking in the Blue," even from the "house of the 'mentally ill.' "

Some critics believe Lowell opens himself to the influence of William Carlos Williams in freeing his verse, and to that of his own student, W. D. Snodgrass, in devising confessional forms of his own. This is moot. But it is certain that Lowell has come into a versatile mood. He produces another volume, *Imitations* (1961), in which he renders poems by Sappho, Propertius, Villon, Baudelaire, Rimbaud, Rilke, and Montale, among others, "one voice running through many personalities." He also completes a translation of Racine's *Phaedra* (1961) and writes verse plays, *The Old Glory* (1964, 1965).

Lowell begins to strike his major note. In *For the Union Dead* (1964) he confronts all the burning themes of the times—faith, history, love, death in all its savage and servile forms—with casual grandeur. Informally, he takes the measure of the world in the breath of a line—"we have talked our extinction to death"—the turn of a metaphor; he reduces the world in the scale of irony and thus looms larger, impersonal confessor. Each poem, supremely *made*, judges Time, as does the title poem or "Jonathan Edwards in Western Massachusetts," the two longest pieces in this work.

Lowell next publishes *Near the Ocean* (1967), illustrated by Sidney Nolan; and *Notebook: 1967–68* (1969), which Lowell describes as "one poem, jagged in pattern, but not a conglomeration or sequence. . . . My plot rolls with the seasons. The separate poems are opportunist and inspired by impulse. Accident threw up subjects, and the plot swallowed them—famished for human chances." Addressed to the events of the day—the Vietnam war, the Newark riots, Che Guevara's death, the murders of Martin Luther King and Robert Kennedy, the French student uprisings—and dedicated to renowned figures, the best poems stubbornly engage the senseless contingency of all our lives in a language of new-felt complexity, though some are oblique and merely knowing, grotesque in their levity. An expanded edition of this work appears in 1970, including new poems held together almost as casually as in a loose leaf folder.

In some peculiar sense, the work of Robert Lowell seems a miraculous anachronism: it represents the heroic effort of Poesy to aver its excellence though it can not vouch for the survival of man. In some odd sense, too, the work is both eschatological and retrograde: it foresees no possibilities for human life that the past has not made explicit in its high forms. The outrage of Lowell can issue in no prophecy but dementia or doom. Nature he scarcely understands, and in America he feels ill at ease. Yet Lowell will be remembered as one of its poets. He knows the terrible struggle that yields the great moment of resolution, and he permits the poet to say what no one knew was his to tell.

PROMINENT POETS

Theodore Roethke

Although Theodore Roethke (1908–1963) is born a few years earlier than most of the major postwar poets, his first book of verse, *Open House* (1941), appears during the war, and his subsequent achievement proves him very much part of the contemporary world. His is an extraordinary achievement, recognized gradually, attaining full recognition posthumously with *The Collected Poems* (1966).

Roethke feels close to the Romantics, Blake, John Clare, Wordsworth, Whitman, Yeats. He distrusts reason, "that dreary shed"; he chooses to proclaim the "condition of joy" in the universe; and he knows as well the "purity of pure despair." He is, perhaps above all else, a poet of Nature, which he knows meticulously and in all its secret and sensuous forms, Nature spiritualized, an Orphic poet who becomes what he sees in sacramental celebration of the unity of all things: "And everything comes to One." He grows up in the shade of a greenhouse his parents tend in Saginaw, Michigan; it later becomes his "symbol of the whole of life."

Yet Nature does not by itself define Roethke's sensibility, both tortured and naïve, so human and animal. He is also a poet of the unconscious, of childhood, leaning to beginnings, clutching for roots; he returns farther back than where life began, to start again; and like many Romantics, he reaches for death. He is a dream poet, wishing his way everywhere; a love singer, sensual and pure; an author of nonsense verse and childhood lyrics. A bare Self—"I'm naked to the bone"—undergoing journeys to the interior, moving outward toward a woman, an animal, a flower, speaks in rhythms of its own.

His earliest work is spare, minimal, the poems tight and brief. Roethke dislikes the obscure intellectual idiom of modernism; he wants the poet to "scorn being 'mysterious' or loosely oracular, but be willing to face up to genuine mystery. His language must be compelling and immediate. . . . " This is true of his second volume, *The Lost Son and Other Poems* (1948), in which the final sequence, exploring the strange movements of the human psyche, in joy, remembrance, terrible exhaustion, in death and rebirth, has no precedent in American verse. With *Praise to the End* (1951)

and especially *The Waking* (1953), Roethke develops his
meditative powers in longer poems, interior monologues, dialectic and dramatic passages, preternatural reveries, varying
in line length, elliptic in syntax, colloquial, richly associative.
Freudian, or perhaps more distinctly Jungian, forms of intuition into previous states of consciousness abound. Yet love
also has a part, as *Words for the Wind* (1958, 1961) mar-
velously shows, in connecting self to other, the I to the world.
So has humor, which plays through the unforgettable rhymes
and retorts of the "Nonsense Poems," in *I Am! Says the Lamb*
(1961).

The last poems, *The Far Field* (1964), gather Roethke's
purpose in wider reflective forms. "A man learning to sing,"
he also asks questions about final things, seeking light, seeking acceptance of Being. Writing in a longer line, a meter
between lyric and prose, his eye close on the object, he recalls both Whitman and Lawrence. "We need," he says,
"the catalogue in our time." He offers far more than a catalogue in "Sequence, Sometimes Metaphysical"; he offers a
dark drive toward God, Oneness. There are moments when
Roethke comes too close to the great authors who influenced
his work; when his poetry gives itself to clichés of doxology;
or when the focus of his insight, excluding much of the human world, seems too special. These moments are infrequent.
More often, he is a poet of the indicative; being, not doing,
is his joy. He is the recipient of some aboriginal magic,   ✓
nature-blessed, master of some hysteria no Word can allay.
He is, finally, a true original who may not shape American
verse, yet henceforth must occupy a unique place in the
soul of poetry.

John Berryman

The poetry of John Berryman (1914–1972) undergoes several transformations in three decades, and in its last phase,

The Dream Songs (1969), takes an extraordinary turn. Berryman is a difficult poet from the start, willful, learned, ironic, a brawling soul exceedingly vulnerable to the degeneracy of the years. He is an American poet, too, full of the history, the language, and the grief of his land. He has an unappeasable conscience, responding to the West's decline with strains and torsions of his own verse, a vision lucid even in derangement. Like Roethke, Berryman believes that "Dissociation often precedes a new state of clarity." Like so many writers of this age, he knows a loneliness more somber than despair, intractable joy, the absolute nakedness of man.

By his own admission, the earliest models of his poetry are Yeats and, somewhat later, Auden; both "saved me," he says, "from the then crushing influences of Ezra Pound and T. S. Eliot." His first books, *Poems* (1942) and *The Dispossessed* (1948), have a deep brooding tone, wrenched syntax and rhythms, a slashing cerebral quality to the line. *Berryman's Sonnets* (1967), written in the Forties and published two decades later, sing of a disastrous love affair. Painfully personal, these pieces still lock the poet within their tortuous structures. But a dramatic concept is beginning to take hold in Berryman's imagination. Character, narrative, and most important, the sense of a shifting, complex point of view, determine his approach; cunningly, he "administers" the pronouns of his verse. The result is a long poem, narrative and meditative, *Homage to Mistress Bradstreet* (1956), sustained by an eight-line stanza and the dominant persona of Anne Bradstreet, who may have been the first Puritan poet of America. Berryman himself moves in and out of the consciousness of his heroine, engages her in dialogue, "a sort of extended witch-seductress and demon-lover bit." The historical character of America and the character of its actuality, the double heritage of Colonial rebellion and submission, struggle to come out of an ambitious work perhaps too heavily mediated by its art.

Despite the great strain of the long poem, Berryman returns to another form of it in 77 *Dream Songs* (1964), to which he later adds *His Toy, His Dream, His Rest* (1968), both collected in *The Dream Songs*. He conceives the dream units in these books—eighteen lines, six-line stanzas, mostly rhymed—as part of a whole poem concerning the "turbulence of the modern world, and memory, and wants," concerning the dramatics of history and its pariahs. The central imaginary character, named Henry, is, according to Berryman, "a white American in early middle age sometimes in blackface, who has suffered an irreversible loss and talks about himself sometimes in the first person, sometimes in the third, sometimes even in the second; he has a friend, never named, who addresses him as Mr. Bones and variants thereof." But Berryman's explanation hardly begins to touch the difficulties, rewards, and subterfuges of the poem, a metaphysical minstrel show full of low comedy and terror and grief, full of "hell-spinning puns" and coarse jokes, allusive, jagged, close to the truth or insanity of dreams. Bored, Henry interrogates the universe with special sound effects; bitter, he makes irreverence into a new kind of justice; breathless, he condemns himself to live. His author, twisting through slang and surrealism, hardly "poetic," subduing his hysteria, yokes the soul of man to things. Beyond quirky style or cranky dream, the songs utter a fundamental cry of existence. They also suggest a way of "constructing" the long poem of our times, a way that is not Eliot's in the *Four Quartets*, Pound's in the *Cantos*, or Williams's in *Paterson*, but at the same time more primitive and mannered, more cute and outrageous in its dissociations of culture, of sensibility.

As a poet, Berryman is extreme; some say he is too obscure, idiosyncratic, deliberately offensive. Yet he creates a unique persona that can "suffer living like a stain," and makes of his poet's "strangeness" a gift to men.

Allen Ginsberg

Perhaps more than any other poet of the period, Allen Ginsberg (born 1926) creates a legend of himself, a series of public figures of odium or adoration. He appears as the Beat Bard, the mad, flailing Genius, the Dionysiac opening sexuality wide, the radical Anarchist, the drugged Prophet of a new consciousness, the obscene Clown, the far Traveler to India, to Japan, to Peru, the bearded Guru of Oriental wisdom, the Jewish Apocalytic crying doom. This means that Ginsberg's poetry is an agent, certainly a part, of a profound cultural transformation in America.

The experiences that go into his poetry are personal, harrowing. Coming from a family of Jewish immigrants, he also grows up with the works of Marx and Lenin; poverty, idealism, hysteria, rule the household. His parents are estranged, his mother—the Naomi of "Kaddish"—terrifyingly, beautifully "mad." She writes him: "The key is in the window, the key is in the sunlight at the window—I have the key. . . . " Ginsberg learns about drugs, insanity, homosexuality, the sheer violence of life, about anger, sweetness, and lamentation. He also has inner strength, vast book knowledge. At Columbia University he studies with Lionel Trilling and Mark Van Doren and becomes acquainted with writers— William Burroughs, Jack Kerouac, Gregory Corso, among others—who give the Beat Movement its shape. Thereafter, he gives himself to various worldly or vatic causes with shrewdness, generosity, boundless energy.

Ginsberg finds his poetic models in Whitman, the blatant and outrageous psalmist rather than the "good grey poet"; in William Carlos Williams, who writes an introduction to Ginsberg's first work, *Howl, and Other Poems* (1956); in the "spontaneous bop prosody" of Kerouac and the "breath" measure of Charles Olson; in "extreme rhapsodic wails" heard in madhouses; in rippling sounds of sacred mantras, sutras, biblical texts. But his true source, he frequently insists, is inspiration, divine possession, the music of the spheres. "Who denies the music of the spheres denies poetry," he writes, "denies man, & spits on Blake, Shelley, Christ & Buddha. Meanwhile have a ball. The universe is a new flower. America will be discovered. Who wants a war against roses will have it."

But against the need for ecstacy stand other ragged needs. When Ginsberg begins to publish in the Fifties, memories of Hitler and Stalin are alive, and McCarthyism is rampant through the early Eisenhower years. There is cause for outrage. Consent and fury—with time, Ginsberg shows more consent than fury—go into the making of "Howl," which begins with the now famous line: "I saw the best minds of my generation destroyed by madness, starving hysterical naked." At its best, the long shuddering lines of this and other poems sustain lyric sob and cosmic howl, humor and rant. Hassidic in perception, obscene in diction—the defeat of censors in court helps to sell over 100,000 copies of the book—the poems address a world crumbling with hatred, fear, an America bestridden by Moloch. Thus Ginsberg, like Lowell, Berryman, and, soon after, Sylvia Plath, embodies the disorders of civilization in his own disorders, "listening to the Terror through the wall," listening also to the voice of the Burning Bush.

In a sense, the work of Ginsberg denies the poem as made object, as artifact; it is a spiritual process, illumination, "complete statement of Person," "self-prophetic" command, or simply Poesy. "Don't hide the madness," he cries. Critical norms tend, therefore, to fail his critics. Still, his poems vary greatly in appeal, power, or inspiration. *Kaddish* (1961), for instance, contains some of his best work; *Reality Sandwiches* (1963, 1966), its poems written a decade earlier, seems less certain, less satisfying; *T. V. Baby Poems* (1968) and *Planet*

News (1968) have syntactic subtlety, music and hallucination. The latter includes the wonderful long poem, "Wichita Vortex Sutra" which Ginsberg describes as "a short fragment of longer trans-american voyage poetries . . . composed directly on tape by voice, and then transcribed to page: page arrangements notates the thought-stops, breath-stops, runs of inspiration, changes of mind, startings and stoppings of the car." People, places, politics, psychedelics, ecology, love, nature, and war are among the concerns of Ginsberg in all these books, journals of a turned-on psyche, mediated little by conscious form, yet shaped by breath and vision, oracular, mantic, surreal, naked.

Some of Ginsberg's poems can be complacent, sentimental, boring; they appeal to a small part of the mind and leave the rest dozing. Others are written, as he says, in Heaven. On the whole, his work attests to the immensity of Is; his concept of Poesy reclaims an ancient fullness. More immediately, his language gives writers new daring and awe in verbal freedom.

TYPES AND TRENDS
OF POETRY

Variations of Formalism

The earliest trend in contemporary poetry embraces variations of the closed style. Gradually, these closed styles evolve toward more open or experimental forms; yet their original derivation from the tradition of Pound-Eliot endows them with a quality, perhaps academic, that they never quite lose. Excellent poets representing many variations of formalism have otherwise little in common. Their work nonetheless conditions the taste of audiences in the first decade after the war.

One of the most accomplished of these poets, Elizabeth Bishop (born 1911) displays from the start, in *North and South* (1946), freshness of imagery, high precision of the mind, idiosyncratic taste. A New Englander by birth, she also spends a good deal of time in Key West and Brazil, places that enrich her vision. Yet the colors of her verse are ultimately intellectual, exact hues of a world full of concrete things, like Marianne Moore's, and flat cadences. Her own objectivity in discerning the aspects and relations of things is visual, and so clear as to be dream-like, fantasmic like some imaginary iceberg, "jewelry from a grave" sparring with the sun. Impeccable in craftsmanship, her second volume, *Poems* (1955), proves her to be a poet's poet, not prolific but ineluctable in her finest work, witty and graceful in the rest, a quiet moralist withal.

J. V. Cunningham (born 1911), lapidary and satiric, seems accomplished in a more limited area of human sensibility. His many volumes include *The Helmsman* (1942), *The Judge Is Fury* (1947), *The Exclusions of a Rhyme* (1960), and *Collected Poems and Epigrams* (1971), which reveal a precise, compressed idiom, traditional verse forms—mostly couplets and rimed quatrains—cutting wit. His inspiration often comes from Roman and Neo-Classical models, though in neat savagery and humor the agonies of his verse are still modern.

Delmore Schwartz (1911–1966) offers the contrast of a passionate temper. A native of Brooklyn, he soon makes a place for himself, with short stories, poems, plays, criticism, and translations of Rimbaud, in the leading quarterlies of New York and becomes himself an editor of *Partisan Review*. His early efforts are quickly recognized for their energy, their resourcefulness. *In Dreams Begin Responsibilities* (1938)—which derives its title from a poem by Yeats, and includes a superb story, a play, and some verse— Schwartz tries to supplant older styles of the Twenties and Thirties without entirely succeeding. His concerns, time, love, the noumenal and phenomenal worlds, are expressed with precocious ease, the music sensuous, the mind playful and philosophic.

In subsequent volumes, too, Schwartz experiments with mixed forms: *Shenandoah* (1941), a play in prose and verse; *Genesis, Book One* (1943), a long narrative poem with chorus; *Vaudeville for a Princess, and Other Poems* (1950), a miscellany. His driving spirit carries its heavy intellectual baggage of myth, history, theology, opera, and film without buckling, seeking, questioning art and questioning life again, knowing what every actor knows, the "contradiction in every act." When the spirit does finally buckle, in despondency, fastidiousness, and self-derision, Schwartz lapses into silence. His great promise unfulfilled, he leaves in *Summer Knowledge* (1959, 1967) the best work of his later, desperate years. The posthumous *Selected Essays of Delmore Schwartz* (1970) proves him to be one of the finest, most versatile men of letters of his generation. Awed in his youth by the great masters of modernism—Joyce, Yeats, Rilke, Eliot, Proust—he reaches for the postmodern spirit, and finds no time to define it.

The impact of Randall Jarrell (1914–1965) also owes much to the very great breadth of his knowledge, his genius as a teacher as well as a critic. His essays, in *Poetry and the Age* (1953), are crucial in interpreting old and new poets to students of literature; his insights into contemporary culture, in *A Sad Heart at the Supermarket* (1962), are both astringent and funny; and *The Third Book of Criticism* (1969) reveals his special talent for eulogy, his infectious sense of wonder and delight in reading literature. Early in his career, at Vanderbilt University, Jarrell comes under the influence of the Fugitives, Ransom in particular, and shares some of their social and formalist views. His own poetry, however, tends to be more colloquial, at once speculative and simple.

His first volumes of verse, *Blood for a Stranger* (1942), *Little Friend, Little Friend* (1945), *Losses* (1948), reflect his war experiences. Jarrell, who serves in the Air Force and recalls bombing missions, soldiers writing home, extermination camps, wrote about these with terrible poignancy, coming close to sentimentality at times, cultivating the commonplace, saved always by a marvelous intelligence which turns a discrete event into a symbolic human and historical statement. His themes include death, loss, failure; his brusque and wry rhythms convey pity; his style, seeking simplicity, flatness, refuses all the seductions of style. In his later work, *The Woman at the Washington Zoo* (1960), *The Lost World* (1965), Jarrell turns to broad dramatic representations of individuals caught in the pathos and horror of a world no saner in peace than in war. Compassion matches the brilliance of his mind; his satire respects pain or innocence. When the *Complete Poems* (1969) appears, it is easy to agree with Lowell that Jarrell is "the most heartbreaking . . . poet of his generation." A part of him possesses childhood eternally, exuberantly, sadly, as his four books for children show.

Clearly, the temper of the best poets associated with formalism is far from sterile; it has, in fact, a sacramental side as the work of Jarrell hints. Other poets give evidence of their natural piety, their alertness to the world. Isabella Gardner (born 1915), for instance, is quietly, wondrously sensitive to the mysteries of human relations, the connections between animals and people, the "service of the universe." Her verse, in *Birthdays from the Ocean* (1955), *The Looking Glass* (1961), and *West of Childhood* (1965), strikes melodies almost Elizabethan in exuberance and control; and her feminine felicity bears continual witness to the person of flesh and bone.

Howard Nemerov (born 1920), is the author of such lively novels as *Federigo, or the Power of Love* (1954) and *The*

Homecoming Game (1957) as well as fine criticism, *Poetry and Fiction* (1963), *Reflexions on Poetry and Poetics* (1972). His books of poetry, from *The Image of the Law* (1947) to *The Blue Swallows* (1967), move from resourcefulness and formal shrewdness to a bolder idiom, concealing toughness and complexity. Skill, humor, terror are always in evidence. Yet Nemerov can also touch the fluidity beneath the earth, seeing and saying "certain simplicities" of life, letting nature speak mysteriously through language, attentive and obedient.

It is Richard Wilbur (born 1921), however, who is most often considered the epitome of formalist grace. Ceremonial, detached, allusive, a craftsman of beauty and scope, he masters various complicated verse forms, from riddles and alliterative verse to sonnets and *ballades*. Emulated for his sensuous symmetries, his Olympian wit, the supreme tact of his best work, Wilbur exerts a certain influence during the Fifties, encouraging sometimes bland restraint. His distrust of the darker and more dangerous reaches of the spirit inhibits his achievement; with time, his closed style loses favor; and Wilbur himself quietly seeks another voice.

Eliot himself recognizes the distinctive note of Wilbur in *The Beautiful Changes* (1947). *Ceremony, and Other Poems* (1950) and *Things of This World* (1956), which contain some of his best poems, follow. Celebration of quotidian things, the illusionism of art, the whimsical epiphanies of men are among his concerns. His classic, comic sense finds an outlet in superb translations and adaptations from the French: *The Misanthrope* (1955), *Candide: A Comic Opera* (1957) with Lillian Hellman and Leonard Bernstein, and *Tartuffe* (1963). With *Advice to a Prophet* (1961), Wilbur begins to change his manner; the poems, still urbane, exhibit a rougher texture, new strength and also new faltering. *Walking to Sleep* (1969), which contains many translations, gives no clear sense of his direction as a poet. It sometimes appears as if his temperament is finally too guarded or fastidious to engage the fullest life of the age.

In the poetry of Daniel Hoffman (born 1923), the ceremonious stance is only one among many. It is most conspicuous in his earliest work, *An Armada of Thirty Whales* (1954) and *A Little Geste* (1960). But in more recent volumes, *Striking the Stones* (1968) and *Broken Laws* (1970), Hoffman insists on engaging experience continuously, shaking loose of decorous abstractions, trying to maintain his own original civility, yet perceiving the ferocity of nature or the abysm that myth hardly conceals. Thus, he ends, in bleak and strong rhythms, by composing a poetry of renunciation, straining "toward another border," where silence frames "the essential psalm." With the full awareness of a scholar-poet, he writes fine critiques, which include studies of Yeats, Muir, and Graves, called *Barbarous Knowledge* (1967), and *Poe, Poe, Poe, Poe, Poe, Poe, Poe* (1972).

The variations of formalism are obviously very considerable, and lack nothing in quality. Almost all the poets in this group are professors; yet their profession hardly imposes unity on their manner. Other poets—they are too numerous to discuss here, though some should be mentioned: Edgar Bowers, Anthony Hecht, John Hollander, Richard Howard, Donald Justice, William Meredith, James Merrill, Howard Moss, Adrienne Rich, Louis Simpson, William Jay Smith, May Swenson, Peter Viereck, Theodore Weiss, Reed Whittermore—further amplify the range of closed styles. But it is true, as James Dickey puts it, that among the lesser academic poets, "Painfully contrived arguments in rhyme substituted for genuine insight."

The Black Mountain Poets

During the early Fifties, an extraordinary confluence of talent appears at Black Mountain College in North Carolina.

Many become known later as leaders of the artistic avant-garde in numerous fields: John Cage (music), Josef Albers (painting), Buckminster Fuller (architecture), Robert Rauschenberg (painting), Merce Cunningham (dance), David Tudor (music), M. C. Richards (pottery). The group also includes poets: Charles Olson, Robert Creeley, Robert Duncan, who are on the staff of the experimental college; and Edward Dorn, Joel Oppenheimer, and Jonathan Williams, who study there. Two magazines, *Black Mountain Review* and *Origin,* serve as an outlet to these poets and attract others, like Denise Levertov, Paul Blackburn, and Paul Carroll—later the editor of *Big Table*—who are not formally associated with the college. The influence of the group is slow in spreading; its members publish mainly in pamphlets put out by private presses or ephemeral magazines and is, therefore, ignored by the establishment of letters for many years.

Indubitably, the central figure of the group is Charles Olson (1910–1970), who serves as rector of Black Mountain College from 1951 to 1956. His affinities are with the poetic tradition of Whitman and Williams, the Pound of the ideograms and *Pisan Cantos,* Louis Zukovsky and his open forms. But Olson, like Duncan or Dorn, is also prodigiously learned in wayward things; he makes original use of geology and geography, myth and history, astronomy and anthropology. His poems, written for his own speaking voice, spoken in fact to students and friends, have a special style, unfinished, telegraphic, scattered like letters or lecture notes; the poems are not meant, as Donald Davie astutely notes, for Empsonian scrutiny. Davie and Charles Tomlinson, in England, follow the lead of the Black Mountain, the San Francisco, and the Beat poets in heeding Olson's manifesto, "Projective Verse."

"Projective Verse" first appears in *Poetry New York* (1950); but it is only when Donald Allen reprints it in his anthology,

The New American Poetry (1960), that it catches the public eye. Olson insists that "form is never more than an extension of content," and urges "composition by field," as "opposed to inherited line, stanza, over-all form." He conceives the poem as a high-energy construct seeking discharge; and demands that each perception lead immediately to a fuller perception. "MOVE, INSTANTER, ON ANOTHER!" he cries. Above all, he contributes a number of technical observations on "breath," the measure of syllable and line and composition. "Breath" serves to give a natural life to each part of the poem, to emphasize the kinetic participation of form in the objects of reality, to recover the "full relevance of human voice." Olson concludes that Projective Verse, if practiced long enough, will permit poets to carry material larger than they have carried since the Elizabethans, permit them to reclaim Truth and Magnitude. Written with eccentric passion, unoriginal in some of its assertions, Olson's essay is still crucial. It expresses the rhapsodic need of poets, enhances the participation of audiences in the poetic act, and declares the poem itself to be a simultaneous presentation of verities, seemingly discrete or discontinuous perhaps, yet within its open form constituting a truth montage. Certain myths of America, of the openness of its time as well as space, lie behind the essay, which implies that literature is much less an institution than a process. Still, Projective Verse lends itself to vast individual variations, the "Hebraic-Melvillian bardic breath" of Ginsberg, the gnostic and visionary verse of Duncan, the wry reticences of Creeley, the elemental simplicity of Snyder.

In Olson's own poetry, complex typographic variations, rhythmic breaks of the line from within or without, collages of quotations, are submitted to the lyric control of "breath," to the underlying mystic chant. His major themes, in *The Distances* (1960), are change, ancient cultures moving or dying, the collapse of human configurations of meaning, modes of the spirit in their physical setting. Ponderous, humorous, self-deprecating, slapdash, Olson leads his readers on a heroic journey. In *The Maximus Poems* (1960) and *Maximus Poems IV, V, VI* (1969), he makes his native Gloucester, Massachusetts, the focus of time and place. As a fishing village, it stands for the origin of culture, which Olson associates with fishing more than hunting, and stands also as a coordinate in the migration of symbols to the West. Written as letters from Maximus—Olson's "Figure of Outward" and "The Man in the Word"—the poems sing the failure or triumph of life, the shifts of ocean and earth, decline in America, the mythic and the aesthetic shapes of creation. In the end, Olson proves a seminal rather than a major poet. The author of a brilliant work on *Moby Dick*, entitled *Call Me Ishmael* (1947), and of curious essays, *The Human Universe* (1965, 1967), he opens up remote perspectives of the mind. His difficult verse is a sourcebook of nature as of imagination.

The affinities of Denise Levertov (born 1923) are with Olson, Duncan, and Creeley, though her own verse, personal and quiet, seems closest to Creeley's. Born in England into a family with a mystic and Hassidic tradition, she takes particular interest in Martin Buber; it is his "Thou" that the reader often feels alive in her work. Her development, under the influence of Williams and H. D. as well as the Black Mountain group, can be seen in the contrast between *The Double Image* (1946), published while she is still resident in England, and *Here and Now* (1957) which reflects her American experience. The form of the later poems seems broken, bits and pieces, yet still wholly harmonious within. Her subsequent work, *The Jacob's Ladder* (1961), *O Taste and See* (1964), proves her mastery of certain spiritual ventures, uttered simply as in prosaic dreams. Writing about marital love or sensuous objects, her imagination meshes into the ambiguous order of reality on some deep level of art.

Her forms, though organic, make way for gaps of perception, keep the rifts open. She says: "The X factor, the magic, is when we come to these rifts and make those leaps. A religious devotion to the truth, to the splendor of the authentic, involves the writer in a process rewarding in itself; but when that devotion brings us to undreamed abysses and we find ourselves sailing slowly over them and landing on the other side—that's ecstasy."

Robert Creeley (born 1926) is ecstatic and enigmatic in a different way. His poems are usually of the "minimal" kind: brief, short-lined, laconic, open to the indeterminacy of the blank page. But their wry humor and reveries conceal intense feeling about living "as we can, each day another," wasting nothing. Their subtle concentration of familiar details, their sly broken music, their diction chosen to slide on the syntax, distinguish the personal lyrics of *For Love* (1962), a collection of two earlier books. *Words* (1967) and *Pieces* (1969) reveal Creeley in a more risky mood. He creates partial patterns; recurrence, remembrance, conventional rhyme, all the elements of relation or conclusiveness, he resists. "Only disconnect": that is his motto, the very stutter in his reading voice. The fragments of language—as of love, of experience generally—address the void. At its worst, the poetry seems too narrow and constricting in spirit. At its best, it is a genuine poetry of silences, of islands left for other island shores. (Creeley is also the author of a novel called *The Island* [1963].) His sense of improvised order is peculiar to himself, beginning with an "inherent periodicity in the weights and durations of words," developing, as in the music of Charlie Parker, with an "intensive variation on 'four-square' patterns. . . . " Like Olson, Creeley insists on "returning to poetry its relation with the *physiological* condition."

Less known than Olson, Levertov, or Creeley, Edward Dorn (born 1929) begins by sharing the expansive tendencies of Olson. In *Geography* (1965) and *The North Atlantic Tur-*

bine (1967), Dorn discovers a kingdom of the imagination among the facts of archaeology, climatology, oceanography, anthropology, "not didactically," Donald Davie notes, "but more freely and provisionally, as a sort of serious make-believe." His later work, *Gunslinger* (Book I & II, 1968, 1969) moves in a new direction, abandoning locality and extension for "that non-spacial dimension, intensity," which Dorn explores in a tone of comic surrealism.

No literary school can, or should, attain complete unity; thus the open styles of the Black Mountain poets remain plural. Writers younger than Olson, such as Paul Blackburn, Paul Carroll, Jonathan Williams, John Wieners, and Joel Oppenheimer, strike distinct notes.

The San Francisco Poets

The poetic scene in San Francisco during the middle and late Fifties is even more diversified. In the cafés, bookshops, and "pads" of the North Shore, literature is authored or argued, verse is sold or sung. Kenneth Rexroth serves as dean of the writers who come flocking to the new bohemia and as their chief polemicist. The new poets—some natives of the city, others late comers to it—have no single program or persuasion other than their distaste for academic formalism. The Beats, the Black Mountain teachers, poets from the East or Northwest, converge for a time to make the "San Francisco Renaissance." Their work appears in magazines such as *Moby, Folder, View, The Ark, Big Table, Yugen, Measure, Contact, San Francisco Review, Northwest Review, Chicago Review, Evergreen Review*; and their books are published by such small presses as City Lights Books, Corinth Books, Auerhahn Press, Jargon Books, Tiber Press, Discovery Books, Toad Press, Totem Press, Coyote Books, White Rabbit Press, and by the well-established Grove Press and New

Directions, both in the East. Their audiences tend to be cultural rebels, youthful enthusiasts.

Brother Antoninus (born 1912), a lay Dominican born William Everson, comes from Sacramento, California, though his raging poetry, enhanced by a Dionysian style of reading, first becomes known in San Francisco. Writing in the great tradition of Spanish baroque ecstasy, of possession and confession, guilt and sensuality, he cries from the depths: "I am burned black." Sometimes his early work seems a cross of Whitman and Hopkins, a nature poem tortured in sound and spirit; and the influence of Robinson Jeffers can also be discerned in the long loose lines of *The Residual Years* (1948). Antoninus struggles with the "core of existence caught on the tongue," coining words, roughing up the "importunate utterance of millions of men." In later work, *The Crooked Lines of God* (1959), *The Hazards of Holiness* (1962), *The Rose of Solitude* (1967), the religious and biblic accents become primary. Claiming no more perfection for art than man can claim for his soul, Antoninus refuses surrender to anything other than his God. Intense as it is ultimate, at times shrill, his poetry seeks the somber ground of absolution and "something very near to annihilation," he says, something akin to spiritual violence for and against God.

But the central yet contrasting figures of the San Francisco Renaissance are Duncan and Ferlinghetti. It is as plausible to place Robert Duncan (born 1919) among the Black Mountain poets as it is right to locate him in the Bay Area —he is born in Oakland—where his impact finally becomes felt. Brilliant of mind and curious of learning, he finds his inspiration among other poets, inevitably Pound, Williams, and H. D., but also such contemporaries as Jack Spicer and Helen Adam, balladeer of the marvelous; among such musicians as Satie, Stravinsky, Schönberg; among painters, both the old masters and the San Francisco Post-Expressionists. Yet his inspiration runs wilder among ancient creation myths, mystical texts like *The Zohar*, fairy tales, treatises of magic, astrology, alchemy. A gnostic by temperament, in search always of the fabulous or numinous, he pursues the creative spirit in its various embodiments, offering a typology of soul. "Where there is soul," he writes, "all the world and body become the soul's adventure. . . . Soul is the body's dream of its continuity in eternity—a wraith of mind. Poetry is the very life of the soul: the body's discovery that it can dream. And perish into its own imagination."

Despite Duncan's admiration for Projective Verse, his own seems restrained, often dense, hermetic except in melody. His early works—illustrated by Jess Collins, who prompts Duncan to experiment with collage techniques—are privately printed. *Selected Poems* (1959) indicates the range of his poetic complexity as of his quirks and mannerisms. More impressive, *The Opening of the Field* (1960) and *Roots and Branches* (1964) develop his central themes: immanence, mythopoesis, homosexual love, despondency. "Our consciousness," he says, "and the poem as a supreme effort of consciousness, come in a dancing organization between personal and cosmic identity." The method of the poems is far more musical than dramatic; for music, the author believes, moves at the heart of nature. Aesthetic, erotic, mystical, the poetry of Robert Duncan wants to create itself from the intellectual order not of one mind but of existence; it does not always succeed.

The poetry of Lawrence Ferlinghetti (born 1919) is far more exoteric. Born in New York, he settles in San Francisco in 1951; and through his City Lights Bookshop and Press contributes vigorously to the emergent literary movement, publishing many works by new writers, including Ginsberg's *Howl*. The oral quality of Ferlinghetti's verse, whether colloquial or declamatory, makes it suitable to café readings, often to the accompaniment of jazz. "I've used 'open-form' typography," he says, "to indicate the breaks and hesitancies of speech as I hear it in the poem. . . . " Socially conscious, politically engaged, satiric, he writes poems with such titles as "Tentative Description of a Dinner Given to Promote the Impeachment of President Eisenhower." In his books, *Pictures of the Gone World* (1955), *A Coney Island of the Mind* (1958), *Starting from San Francisco* (1961), Ferlinghetti is irreverent, humorous, mundane. Yet, putting aside the clownish guise, he can burst into sudden anger at sham or injustice, burst with the authentic power of poetry. Like E. E. Cummings or Kenneth Patchen before him, he can convert extravagant wit or protest into some human perception of wonder and generosity. Unhappily, the loud publicist in him sometimes prevails. Ferlinghetti also writes a novel, *Her* (1961), and some short experimental plays, *Routines* (1964).

Not all the native poets of the Bay Area are closely associated with the San Francisco Renaissance. James Schevill (born 1920), a prolific poet and dramatist born in Berkeley, remains somewhat eccentric to the movement. Though his earlier works, *Tensions* (1947) and *The American Fantasies* (1951), reflect the formalism of the period, he is too vital, too independent a poet to suffer the containments of that manner. His later works, *Stalingrad Elegies* (1964), *Violence and Glory* (1969), *Lovecraft's Follies* (1971), are full of experiments, dramatic, typographic, musical.

Philip Lamantia (born 1925) engages himself, for a time, with both the San Francisco and Beat movements. Born in San Francisco, later a resident of Seattle, he also edits *View* magazine, which publishes some remarkable verse in a wild open style. Initially a Surrealist, hailed by André Breton himself, Lamantia turns to an incantatory poetry full of mystic celebrations and "ekstasis." His works, from *Erotic Poems* (1946) and *Narcotica* (1959) to *Selected Works 1943–1966* (1967) and *Blood of the Air* (1970), prove him to be a poet of pythagorean wisdom, hallucinatory images, lines contracting and expanding into prose paragraphs freely.

Other poets of the original San Francisco Renaissance include James Broughton, Jack Spicer, Madeline Gleason,
Robin Blaser. But as new poets come on the scene, the movement becomes increasingly heterogeneous, spreading to various parts of the country.

Beats, Nature Mystics, and Others

The paths of the Beat and San Francisco writers cross in
time, in place, and in poetic mind; their personal friendships,
their life styles, their vehement rejection of formalism and
middle-class values serve as common ground. Yet the Beats
also have a separate identity. The initial associations of Jack
Kerouac, Allen Ginsberg, Gregory Corso, William Burroughs
are in New York. The Beat poets drift in and out of San
Francisco, joining Gary Snyder, Philip Whalen, and Michael
McClure in readings there; and they also publish in *Black
Mountain Review*. Their spirit is antic, reckless, at times
violent. Crime, madness, drugs, anarchy are elements of
their experience, and so are the sacred texts of the world.
Blasphemy and obscenity are expressions of their revolt and
of their search for beatitude. Their heroes are the usual
masters of the open style, from Whitman to Williams, and
the visionary poets, from Blake and Rimbaud to Artaud.
  More immediately, the Beats admire Kenneth Patchen
(1911–1972), who works in steel mills and coal mines in
his youth, and writes a special vernacular, mixing prose and
poetry, surrealism and revolution, humor and horror. His
numerous works, which include *First Will & Testament*
(1939), *The Dark Kingdom* (1942), *Cloth of the Tempest*
(1943), *Memoirs of a Shy Pornographer* (1945), and *Red
Wine and Yellow Hair* (1949), reveal a phantasmagoric
world, violent, ugly, obscene. His improvised forms, his
savagery in satire or outrage, his sympathy for the insulted,

the desolate, "Sleep-walkers in a dark and terrible land," are close to the sympathies of the Beats.

Among older poets, beside Rexroth, the Beats also find a surprising champion in Karl Shapiro (born 1913). His transformation from a disciple of Eliot and Auden, writing in the closed style of *Person, Place and Thing* (1942) and *V-Letter* (1944), into the later truculent poet is striking. There is some evidence even in his early work of jagged perception, a brusque personal idiom, whether he speaks of war or injustice. But Shapiro is also editor for a time of *Poetry*, the stronghold of modernist verse; and his *Essay on Rime* (1945) pleases the academics. The change clearly begins to show in the polemic essays of *Beyond Criticism* (1953) and *In Defense of Ignorance* (1960), in which the author attacks excessive intellectualism, all the literary and cultural dogmas of the age, shifting his allegiances from Eliot to Lawrence, from Auden to Henry Miller. But it is in the rugged, sometimes cranky, verse of *Poems of a Jew* (1958) and, more particularly, of *The Bourgeois Poet* (1964) that Shapiro proves his development. Abandoning rhyme, abandoning even meter, he ends by frankly adopting the prose poem, autobiographic, grotesque, bitterly satiric, awry with energy.

Yet neither Patchen nor Shapiro can be remotely considered as Beat poets. Ginsberg, of course, is the paragon, though he grows into a role that sets him apart; and Kerouac, who writes some poems, is better known for his spontaneous prose. It is Gregory Corso (born 1930), perhaps, who best exemplifies the Beat poet. Born in New York, abandoned by his mother, raised in orphanages and by foster parents, acquainted with reformatories and prisons (including the infamous Tombs of Manhattan), he is first published by the Harvard *Advocate*. He counts Ginsberg among close friends, and later Ferlinghetti, who prints his *Gasoline* (1958). Some poems of that volume seem written with "automaticism," which the author explains as "an entranced moment in which the mind accelerates a constant hour of mind-foolery, mind-genius, mind-madness. . . . " *The Happy Birthday of Death* (1960) mingles impish prophecy with the erotics of death. Yet Corso is essentially a *naif* beneath the hoodlum or wild-man skin, a child of sorrows who never surrenders his faith in man. *Long Live Man* (1962), a kind of hymn to choice and life's variousness, full of paranoia too, projects his swinging and shrieking self into the pure energy of the universe. More often, Corso thrashes about in original ignorance, exhibitionist in pain. Still, his response to vatic and historical realities, in *Elegiac Feelings American* (1970), is denser, more resonant, than in any previous book. His credo, throughout, remains the same: "Poetry is seeking the answer, joy is in knowing there is an answer, and death is knowing the answer."

Gary Snyder (born 1930), who knows many of the Beats personally and even suggests the hero in Kerouac's *The Dharma Bums*, moves closer to nature mysticism than any of them. A native of San Francisco, he works as logger, forest ranger, seaman; and he studies mythology, linguistics, Oriental cultures, spending years in Japan acquiring the discipline of Zen. His poems are influenced by the rhythms of his physical work, by the geology of his environment in the Sierras, Oman, or Kyoto, by Indian folk tales, classical Chinese poetry, or haiku. He believes that "each poem grows from an energy mind field dance, and has its own inner grain. To let it grow, to let it speak for itself, is a large part of the work of the poet." Snyder's own poetry is wholly integral, its body, speech, and mind uniting in free forms. *Riprap* (1959) gives a tranquil, concrete vision of the Northwest landscape, mountains, rivers, trees, a vision predicated on the poet's certainty: "A clear, attentive mind / Has no meaning but that / Which sees is truly seen." *Myths & Texts* (1960) is more ambitious. Standing for the two sources of knowledge, symbol and sensation, the title also refers to a spiritual-ecological-historical system that the various poems explore with wondrous particularity. In some poems, too, Snyder begins a quiet synthesis of Marx and Zen, a politics of nature that appeals to the post-revolutionary sensibility of some youth, and finds its fullest expression in *Revolution within the Revolution within the Revolution* (1970). Naming the names, arranging the sounds with effortless wisdom, relying on nouns and participles of Being, and sometimes on a dramatic structure akin to the Japanese No plays, the poems of *A Range of Poems* (1967) and *The Back Country* (1968) spread slowly through the consciousness of readers. An extraordinary collection of Snyder's notes and queries, *Earth House Hold* (1969), presents his views in a manner more poetic than discursive.

A number of other poets declare their affinities for the Beat and San Francisco movements without belonging completely to either circle. Philip Whalen (born 1923), an Oregonian, publishes in the underground press and little magazines of the Bay Area, though his own sensibility is distinct, is closer to the landscapes of Gary Snyder than to anything else. Nine of his books of poetry are collected in *On Bear's Head* (1969) which includes notes, drawings, typographic variations, myths, learning, fragments of perception, symbols, silences, songs, hallucinations, haiku-like statements, solitude and happiness in the universe. Whalen himself describes his work: "A continuous fabric (nerve movie?) . . . say a few hours of total attention and pleasure . . . causing great sections of his [the reader's] nervous system . . . to LIGHT UP."

Michael McClure (born 1932), a Midwesterner, also finds part of his inspiration among the San Francisco poets, though he notes: "I am close to Lawrence and Melville and I find how much I despise Williams and Pound." His books, from *Passage* (1956) and *For Artaud* (1959) to *Star* (1970), struggle against their abstract tendency, seek release of their emotional energy. "My viewpoint is ego-centric," he notes in 1959. "Self-dramatization is part of a means to belief and Spirit." At times, a kind of self-hatred, of psychic violence —the style of exclamations, capitals, repetitions—gives a forced quality to his work. But there is also suffering in his best poems, and it makes these poems glow.

Still younger poets, like Richard Brautigan, Ron Loewin-sohn, and David Meltzer, show that the Bay Area remains a haven of new literary talent.

The New York Poets

A very different group of poets, intensely cosmopolitan in spirit, forms in New York. Their affinities are with the European avant-garde, going back to Mallarmé and Corbière, Jarry and Apollinaire, Mayakovski, Tzara, and Breton. They are also close to the various circles of Action Painting, the Museum of Modern Art, *Art News*, the Living Theatre, and the Artists' Theatre. Three of them—Kenneth Koch, Frank O'Hara, and John Ashbery—meet at Harvard before coming to New York, where Barbara Guest, James Schuyler, and Edward Field enlarge their circle. Their concept of poetry owes something to the Surrealist image, the theater of the absurd, the free-verse paragraph of contemporary French poetry. But above all, their concept demands a humorous or hallucinatory refusal of sense, stucture, coherence; it relies on a spatial disposition of poetic clues, which invokes a new quality of attention. Their language, so it seems, is all primary colors and play.

Kenneth Koch (born 1925) writes in a state of perpetual excitement, childlike and wily, trying to populate some gorgeous region of language where pleasure and illogic and invention are all one. His first major work, *Ko, or a Season on Earth* (1959), is a monstrous mock epic, a statement on chaos or mutability, on natural glee, on the subversion of poesy by itself. Byron's *Don Juan* and Ariosto's *Orlando Furioso, ottava rima* and a Japanese baseball star, Tahiti and Kalamazoo, are all part of it. Yet, sometimes, the poem's spark jumps from nonsense to ecstasy. *Thank You, and Other Poems* (1962) and *The Pleasures of Peace* (1968) reveal his maniacal will to gaiety, creation, and outrage. Parodying all genres and conventions, Koch seems to spin free both of form and absurdity, celebrating the terror of possibility. As the price of freedom, Koch faces the charge of his readers: that his poems are inexplicable, and some of them unreadable. A collection of his short plays, produced Off-Broadway, is entitled *Bertha* (1966).

Frank O'Hara (1926–1966) cultivates a more prosaic manner, refusing to refine the indiscriminateness of urban life by art. Yet the manner is ultimately sophisticated; and it expresses the desire of a complex personality to find itself, beyond wit or learning, gossip or chic, beyond its own "catastrophe." *Meditations in an Emergency* (1957) and *Lunch Poems* (1965), eschewing rhythm, assonance, and often rhyme, offer an inclusive landscape of modernity, brittle and hard, bright-surfaced here, deathly there. Between self-hatred and fidelity to fact, the poems of O'Hara take their free shape, as free and as constrained as the paintings of his friends Jackson Pollock, Wilhelm de Kooning, and Grace Hartigan (O'Hara serves for a time as a curator of the Musem of Modern Art). "My formal 'stance' is found," he says, "at the crossroads where what I know and can't get meets what is left of what I know and can bear without hatred." There is evidence that the influence of O'Hara is growing among new poets, especially in the East.

But it is John Ashbery (born 1927), perhaps, who possesses the largest mystery. Word-by-word and line-by-line clear, elegant, and sometimes waggish, his poems are so discontinuous, his sense so recalcitrant, as to defy the closure of a "complete" reading, much like a parable by Kafka, a Dadaist joke, a dream. By comparison with his later work, *Turandot, and Other Poems* (1953) and *Some Trees* (1956) seem obedient to conventions of the masters. The change is subtle. *The Tennis Court Oath* (1962), *Rivers and Mountains* (1966), *The Double Dream of Spring* (1970), have an arcane mythology, controlled yet utterly wild; they offer an experience of pure poetry, disquieting and weird. Their author, cold fantasist lost in reality, manages still to evoke feelings of innocence, courtesy, or love. Yet the strange seemliness of Ashbery conceals a kind of savagery. He says of certain types of painting similar to his own poetry: "The only thing you have to hold onto is your own natural savagery, and your ability to recognize your own *natural* savagery has been given to you by this art which in turn is the cause of your anxiety about not being able to recognize anything but yourself." *Yourself!* that is indeed the chimera within Ashbery's art, which every detail seeks to reveal and seeks to disguise. An admirer of Raymond Roussel and Henry Green, artists of the mystery fully particularized, Ashbery takes final refuge from himself in the labyrinthine indifference of the true aesthete, and in the absurdist's contempt for his own art. Author of experimental plays, *The Heroes* (1950), *The Compromise* (1955), editor of *Art News*, a magus of the mind in search of its own deep play, his poetry nonetheless has limited impact on writers outside of his circle.

The New York poets, who count Barbara Guest, James Schuyler, Edward Field, Ted Berrigan, and David Shapiro among their other members, are anti-formalist in a sense, inventors of new open styles. Yet their openness is cryptic; and their aversion to statement, to theme, to directness, betrays a formal concern with the origins of language, the wordless music of consciousness.

The Post-Romantics

No adequate rubric can describe the number of poets who elude the convenience of the previous categories. Yet many of these writers share a certain slant of sensibility, a certain attitude toward the traditions of literature. Their own tradition is largely Romantic, but they also capture the wryness and sharpness and derangement of the contemporary world. That is why we may speak of them as Post-Romantics who push the dialectic of open and closed styles, of formalism and anti-formalism, beyond the old polarities. Eclectic in their inspiration, they find it in Yeats or Williams, Stevens or Pound, Lowell, Roethke, or Olson; and their own verse evolves in independent modes, vital, fluid, or visionary, yet still measured. Very often, they show a mystic awareness of nature. Very often, they choose the confessional mode. Almost always, they speak through some subjective agent, an internal mask, a hidden persona of the Poet. In a sense, then, the Post-Romantics hold the large middle ground, assimilating influences, moving through various phases toward some still unknown future of poetry.

It is hard to see where this Post-Romantic tendency begins. Perhaps it begins as far back as the work of Muriel Rukeyser (born 1913). *Theory of Flight* (1935), *A Turning Wind* (1939), *Beast in View* (1944), and *The Green Wave* (1948) show increasing emancipation from the idioms of formalism. The tone is dramatic, emotional, as in "The Soul and Body of John Brown"; or else it is personal, as in "Effort at Speech Between Two People." The lines are loose and supple, sometimes also flat. The poetry engages the world and its political turmoils, and engages also the more private currents of feeling between people.

But the Post-Romantic element can also be seen in a very different type of poet, William Stafford (born 1914). His is

a quiet, reflective mind, attuned to the mysteries of nature
in the American West, at ease in poetry. His books, from
West of Your City (1960), through *Traveling through the
Dark* (1962) and *The Rescued Year* (1966), to *Allegiances*
(1970), have a marvelous delicacy of accurate perception
which reminds us that "Our duty is just a certain high kind
of waiting." Through the poems, we sense the solitude of
the poet, sense his vast acceptance of how "the world feels
. . . in dear detail / be ideal light all around us." Writing
with intuitive freedom, his "practice initially is to roam
forward through experience, finding the way as the process unfolds." The simplicities of Stafford as he roams the
immense country are—like Gary Snyder's—sacramental,
gestures in a ritual of ancient participation, of continuous
conciliation.

Stafford stands, in some ways, at the edge of contemporary
poetry. The direction of the Post-Romantic trend is better
suggested by James Dickey (born 1923), who says: "Of late
my interest has been mainly in the conclusionless poem, the
open or generalizing poem, the un-well-made poem." His
own poetry, vitalist in origin, incarnates his "best moments,"
which have in them elements of danger, of joy, and of repose.
A Southerner, an accomplished guitarist, an enthusiastic out-
doorsman, a decorated pilot in both World War II and the
Korean War, he knows nature as well as the strange reci-
procities of men and beasts, the pervasiveness of death, the
will to transcendence. Interested initially in poems with a
basic narrative structure, Dickey writes *Into the Stone*
(1960) and *Drowning with Others* (1962), dream and fact
united in a single state of conscience as of consciousness,
sometimes hallucinatory in power. Still struggling with the
guilt and horrible ecstasies of war, he experiments with split
lines and a tone of greater immediacy in *Helmets* (1964).
Buckdancer's Choice (1965) is perhaps his most impressive
volume. Finding no expiation in art for human violence,

Dickey turns the past on the present, the Self toward the Other, nature against man, questioning the cosmic, the moral, the aesthetic order of things. Again, but more insistently than ever, the voice that speaks in *The Eye-Beaters* (1970) is the personal voice seeking spiritual legitimacy, seeking mercy, in a brute and energetic world. Dickey himself moves in the center of the dramatic structure, drawing his readers into a wider act of participation into existence, its tenderness, its malevolence. Prolix at times, given to Faulknerian clichés, too loud in masculine affirmations, Dickey's best poetry still sings with unique lust and integrity. The author of two books of criticism, *The Suspect in Poetry* (1964) and *Babel to Byzantium* (1968), Dickey also writes a smoldering novel of action and reflection, *Deliverance* (1970).

On the surface, John Logan (born 1923) may seem an academic poet—he is a gifted teacher, first at Notre Dame, then at the State University of New York at Buffalo, and the editor of *Choice*—a Catholic professor who brings his theological and literary lore to his verse. But the appearance is deceptive. His work, calculatedly flat, perhaps technically too simple, is also highly personal and inward; and his desire for the absolute takes familiar forms. Tenderness and even pathos mingle with his awareness of love, love as the religious force of existence. In his volumes of poetry, *Cycle for Mother Cabrini* (1955), *Ghosts of the Heart* (1960), *Spring of the Thief* (1963), *The Zig Zag Walk* (1969), Logan writes about obscure Christian saints and martyrs as well as a high school picnic, about Heine or the failings of his own flesh, achieving more and more freedom of voice, achieving at his very best some clear union of transfiguration and autobiography.

There is something of this in the extraordinary poetry of A. R. Ammons (born 1926), who, after writing an obscure volume of verse, *Ommateum* (1955), publishes in quick succession *Expressions of Sea Level* (1964), *Tape for the Turn of the Year* (1965), *Corson's Inlet* (1965), and *Northfield Poems* (1966). Unlike Logan, however, Ammons feels closer to Transcendentalism than to Catholicism; he seeks pure Being *in* the universe. His language, speedy yet prosaic in rhythms, broken on the page in strange patterns as if only thus it could hold and reveal its secrets, refuses external forms. The reader experiences Ammons's meaning in a "dense reserve of silence," in an erotic fullness of mind, or in a sudden access of infinitude. *Uplands* (1970) and *Briefings* (1971) show Ammons's mastery of the short lyric, difficult yet radiant, detached yet uniquely his own, a "handiwork redeemed from chance" that still aspires, like wind or water, never to "survive its motions."

The confessional mode is more pronounced in W. D. Snodgrass (born 1926), whose verse is witty, candid, and self-ironic. His world is essentially the secular world apprehended through autobiography and all its peculiar embarrassments. His first book, *Heart's Needle* (1959), is also one of the first to adopt the stance of self-exposure among poets trained in verbal *politesse*. Though Snodgrass favors regular verse forms, his language is direct, homey in the nuances of American speech, and striking in its sudden personal twists. A student of Lowell and also an admirer of Jarrell, Snodgrass exemplifies the post-formalist as well as the Post-Romantic trend toward individual expression, neither academic nor Beat. Speaking of his love, his divorce, or his own daughter, he manages also to make echoes of the Korean War part of his voice. Impish in humor, complex in his sincerity, still somehow cool, he seeks in his first book to know his "name." "Poets of our generation," he admits, "have such extensive resources for disguising ourselves from ourselves." Disguise, confession, and self-division—these are the curse and cure of Snodgrass, the burden he seeks to depose in *After Experience* (1968). Reaching for some form of reconciliation richer than psychoanalysis can ever afford the indigent ego, he expresses a Self reborn in poems of "blunt beauty," controlled in their new-found release. His talent, however, remains special, his essential contribution to poetry still moot.

Romantic in another vein, Robert Bly (born 1926) calls attention to his poetry as well as to the combative magazine called by each decade, called now *The Seventies*, which he edits with the help of James Wright. Much of Bly's work seems quiet, even flat, nature poetry—he hails from Minnesota—with sudden bursts of surrealist imagery. Crying for a new freedom of association, invoking the passion of Blake and Novalis, he accuses the Black Mountain Poets of a crypto-formalist preoccupation with technique and asks for free expressions of "rebellious energy." "We have not yet regained in American poetry that swift movement all over the psyche, from conscious to unconscious, from a pine table to mad inward desires," he says. His books, *Silence in the Snowy Fields* (1962) and *The Light Around the Body* (1967), reveal what Bly can do when his associative powers and straggling music hit the invisible heights of poetry. Behind many of the simple-seeming, declarative poems lurks the presence of the sixteenth-century German mystic Jakob Böhme, the urge to absolve man of his false identity, released in death. Yet Bly can also write precisely of politics, the degradations of his country, the wars that man makes as if he were annointing himself, as *Forty Poems Touching on Recent American History* (1970) shows. His true spiritual quality, though, is watery, slow, regenerative, running deep beneath the great plains of the Midwest, pushing suddenly through bole and flower; hence the primal accents of his translations from Neruda and Vallejo. The light around the body of his verse is of a body "Not yet born."

A close associate, James Wright (born 1927), Ohioan by birth, visionary of the human, writes mainly a free verse structured only by its parallelisms of syntax and feeling. His first book, *The Green Wall* (1957), influenced by Robert

Frost and Edwin Arlington Robinson, departs from the well-wrought preciocities fashionable among neophytes of the period. In that volume as in his next, *Saint Judas* (1959), Wright chooses a poetry of experience about ordinary events or solitary people, a poetry transformed from within by an intensity that becomes almost frightening in his public readings. Many of the poems, however, are still stanzaic, regular. *The Branch Will Not Break* (1963) establishes him as an original voice speaking of elemental occurrences in a style more direct and colloquial, yet still inward. With Bly and Wright foremost in mind, Donald Hall notes: "This new imagination reveals through images a subjective life which is *general*, and which corresponds to an old objective life of shared experience and knowledge." This sacramental subjectivity, reminiscent of Roethke, complemented by the sacramental objectivity of Gary Snyder and William Stafford, gives the poetry of James Wright strange subliminal force in *Shall We Gather at the River* (1968). Lucid with knowledge of their own depths, the images organize themselves simply around each unstated theme until the reader perceives his own nature reflected in Wright's poem, its lines changing calmly in length, in rhythm, to suit the depths of human need. His *Collected Poems* (1971) convinces the critics of the richness and magnitude of his achievement.

The achievement of W. S. Merwin (born 1927) is more various and certainly as impressive. The confessional element, though present, is muted by larger concerns that he shares, from a certain distance, with both Wright and Bly. Prolific and versatile—he translates with distinction poetry from the Spanish, French, Russian, Latin, and writes verse and prose plays such as *Favor Island* (1957)—Merwin steadily moves toward his own version of an open form, which he describes thus: "A poetic form: the setting down of a way of hearing how poetry happens in words. The words themselves do not make it. At the same time it is testimony of a way of hear-

ing how life happens in time. But time does not make it."
His first book of verse, *A Mask for Janus* (1952), makes an
impression of enchantment and intimate ease. Intricacy and
decorum and mythic sheen are qualities of *The Dancing
Bears* (1954), too, and its vision is one of recurrence in
mutability. But in *Green with Beasts* (1956) and *The Drunk
in the Furnace* (1960), Merwin adopts a more disjunctive,
discursive manner, challenging his Orphic themes, restating
them on deeper levels, "living forward" through the menaces
of nature. His best poems to date are from *The Moving
Target* (1963), *The Lice* (1967), and *The Carrier of Lad-
ders* (1970). Gnomic, abrupt, mysterious, drawing on an
imagination refined by some invisible element of the earth,
Merwin exposes his lines—with little punctuation, with no
cleverness or willfulness—to silence, to some immense freedom akin to prophecy. From Lucretius to René Char, Merwin
finds a poetic wisdom as wide as the universe; but what he
makes of his own nature is uniquely a poetry of his own.

The poetry of Galway Kinnell (born 1927) also finds its
reality in changeful nature, where everything turns upon
itself and death dances with resurrection. Heraclitean and
Christian mysteries fill the moment. Yet at times the romantic
effusions of Kinnell seem too facile, and his pyrotechnics lack
sustained meaning. His first book, *What a Kingdom It Was*
(1960) establishes his ease and richness of language, his
generosity of feeling. *Flower Herding on Mount Monadnock*
(1964) and *Body Rags* (1968) develop his skills toward loose
accentual rhythms, a more uneven music. But the grief of
mortality, the desire for rebirth, the brilliance of nature in
its strange transmutations still haunt him. Seeking always
intensities, pyrophanies or sacred traces, his imagination can
flicker between New York's East Village and a field of golden-
rod. Opening himself exuberantly—becoming the flame as
he goes up in flames—Kinnell gives us his most characteristic poems in a natural language, the sound of the elements

still carrying inflections of human pity. He is also the author of a novel, *Black Light* (1966), and a translator, *The Poems of François Villon* (1965).

Autobiography is far more explicit in the work of Anne Sexton (born 1928). The few joys and more continuous anguish of her New England life thread her poems, one to the other, in *Bedlam and Part Way Back* (1960), *All My Pretty Ones* (1961), *Live or Die* (1967), and *Love Poems* (1969). She speaks clearly, incisively, without self-pity, of physical illness and mental breakdown, of family—especially the mother—lovers, and friends, of religious schooling and tortuous skepticism, of life's endless pain; she tells nearly everything and thus restores herself. Her world, sometimes elegiac, rarely gay, bares all its nerves to the glaring light of her mind, which honors and relishes each fact, each truth. Writing in roughly or remotely rhymed verse paragraphs, Anne Sexton can release private terrors into sudden incantations that readers recognize as their own night song, song of a "starry starry night," tempting us to cry: "This is how / I want to die." Yet unlike other confessional poets—Lowell, with whom she studies, or Sylvia Plath, whose work she knows closely—Anne Sexton has a narrower cultural focus, finally a more conventional manner.

The most exacerbated poet of this Post-Romantic company, however, is undoubtedly Sylvia Plath (1932–1963), who spends the later part of her life in England, married to the poet Ted Hughes. Ailing, inspired, at times mad, she dies by her own hand; and writes verse of grotesque power and originality, macabre in its badinage, bloody in laying the soul bare. *The Colossus* (1960, 1962) reveals her austere sense of herself in bitter dramas of love and dying, in pastorals of decomposition. Taking risks with her great intelligence, she ends by enlarging the apprehension of her subject. She says: "I believe that one should be able to control and manipulate experiences, even the most terrifying

—like madness, being tortured. . . . I think that personal experience shouldn't be a kind of shut box and mirror-looking narcissistic experience. I believe it should be generally relevant to such things as Hiroshima and Dachau, and so on." It is these larger intensities that she brings to *Ariel* (1965, 1966), a superior volume. Its poems range widely; they are about family, love, disease, politics, Christian myth, the poisoning of nature, the contortions of consciousness. Inventive, bizarre, slangy, terrifyingly plain, they move beyond their own center of fear toward some reconciliation in love that Sylvia Plath is never permitted to reach. Yet she bequeaths brilliance, daring of language, a desperate motion of the mind. In his introduction to the American edition of *Ariel*, Lowell writes: "Her art's immortality is life's disintegration." She clamors also for life's renewal, as her novel, *The Bell Jar* (1963), tells.

The Black Poets

The tradition of Black poetry goes back to Paul Laurence Dunbar in the nineteenth century; and it is further developed by James Weldon Johnson and Claude McKay. But its real origins are older, deeper in Black culture, deriving from folk tales, myths, dances; from work songs, the blues, spirituals; from jazz; from words of confidential wisdom passed from father to son and mother to daughter; from the vernacular of jokes. The soul of Black poetry is *sound*, not print or image. With the Harlem Renaissance of the Twenties, the sounds of Black speech enter into more complex literary forms; and the Negro intellectual, though he still stands some distance from his people, begins to realize his role.

Foremost among the poets of that period, and an uneasy influence on postwar poets just as Richard Wright is on postwar novelists, Langston Hughes (1902–1967) voices his ethnic passion in numberless plays, poems, stories, and essays. More than anyone else, he articulates the concept of American Negritude, helping new writers, carrying their cause both at home and abroad, editing such pioneering anthologies as *The Poetry of the Negro, 1746–1949* (1949), *Poems from Black Africa* (1963), and *New Negro Poets: U.S.A.* (1964). His own innovations are manifest in *Selected Poems of Langston Hughes* (1959).

Other poets of Hughes's generation also prepare the way for postwar Black verse. These include Melvin B. Tolson (1900–1966), neglected author of three books: *Rendezvous with America* (1944), *Libretto for the Republic of Liberia* (1953), *Harlem Gallery: The Curator* (1965); Arna Bontemps (born 1902), with Hughes coeditor of *The Poetry of the Negro, 1746–1949* and himself editor of *American Negro Poetry* (1963) and author of *Personals* (1963); Countee Cullen (1903–1946), a lyricist whose best work appears posthumously in *On These I Stand* (1947).

With the emergence of the Black Power Movement in the Sixties, however, a new type of poetry comes into being. It is, of course, more militant and proud. But it is also more communal, gravid with the sense of a Black destiny; its themes are urgent and large. The new poetry springs from the ugly ghettoes of America and takes loudly to the streets. It is elemental as well as revolutionary, more aware of its origins than ever before, more dedicated to the mission of overcoming the double consciousness of Blacks in White America; it is therefore blatant in its aim to build morale, its sheer lust for rhetoric. But the music saves it, the stunning genius of a John Coltrane, Aretha Franklin, Sun Ra, Ray Charles, who give their beats to language. As Larry Neal, coeditor with Imamu Amiri Baraka (LeRoi Jones) of an important anthology called *Black Fire* (1968), puts it:

> We can learn more about what poetry is by listening to the cadences in Malcolm's speeches, than from most of

> Western poetics. Listen to James Brown scream. Ask your-
> self, then: Have you ever heard a Negro poet sing like that?
> Of course not. . . . The key is in the music.

Hence the concept of the poet Neal describes:

> What this has all been leading us to say is that the poet
> must become a performer, the way James Brown is a per-
> former—loud, gaudy, and racy. He must take his work
> where his people are: Harlem, Watts, Philadelphia, Chicago,
> and the rural South. . . . We must make literature move people
> to a deeper understanding of what this thing is all about, to
> be a kind of priest, a black magician, working juju with the
> word on the world.

The ideal of the Black poet as "juju" revolutionary is one
that various writers approach variously. Robert E. Hayden
(born 1913), a professor at Fisk University and winner of
the Grand Prize for Poetry at the First World Festival of
Negro Arts in Dakar (1965), seems controlled in his passion,
sometimes allusive and analytical, sometimes fully responsive
to the folklore of his people, in *A Ballad of Remembrance*
(1962) and *Selected Poems* (1966). Dudley Randall (born
1914), owner of the Broadside Press in Detroit, publishes
many unknown poets in attractive pamphlets. Brooding,
quiet, and craftsmanlike, his own work, in *Poem Counter-
poem* (1966) and *Cities Burning* (1968), adheres generally
to strict forms. Writing and teaching in Chicago for many
years, Gwendolyn Brooks (born 1917) exerts considerable influence on students of poetry. Her books, *A Street in Bronze-
ville* (1945), *Annie Allen* (1949), *Selected Poems* (1963),
give a strong impression of order and concentration, of a
deep, sad, and vivid life.

But the ideal of the "juju" poet is more fully exemplified
by writers still younger in age, closer to the center of the
Black movement. Imamu Amiri Baraka, formerly LeRoi Jones
(born 1934), comes to be one of these. As an editor of

Yugen magazine in New York, his initial associations are
with the Beats; and he admires the Projective Verse of Olson.
His credo, in Donald M. Allen's *The New American Poetry*,
where his work first becomes known, reads in part: "MY
POETRY is whatever I think I am." Baraka, however, moves
rapidly away from white culture. After Zen and the Yoruba
craze, he becomes a Black Muslim and bears an Arabic
name. As a founder of the Jihad Press and Spirit House in
Newark, he works with Black radical artists, the poets
Edward Spriggs and Yusef Iman, the musicians Pharaoh
Saunders and Sun Ra. Baraka's early poetry, *Preface to a
Twenty Volume Suicide Note* (1961), energetic, existential,
open, blasts the sodden or vicious quality of life in middle-
class America. In *The Dead Lecturer* (1964) and *Black Art*
(1966), however, the anger is sharply focused on the racial
thing; the lines sometimes attain strange intensities, sometimes beat the slow rhythm of declarative statements. A connoisseur of jazz, Baraka writes perceptively on the subject
in *Blues People* (1963) and *Black Music* (1967).

The Black Power Movement triggers the creative temper
in various parts of the land. From Indianapolis, the voice of
Mari Evans (born 1923), author of *Where Is All the Music*
(1968), is heard, whimsical, humorous, satirical, confident in
the sufficiency of Blackness. From New York, Audre Lorde
(born 1934), author of *First Cities* (1968), and Sonia Sanchez
(born 1935), who collects her poems in broadsides, *Homecoming* (1969) and *We a Baddddd People* (1970), write
verse of similar intent yet contrasting mood—the first often
lyrical, the second mordant, wicked. An Alabaman by birth,
Julia Fields (born 1938) teaches and composes accomplished
verse which appears in various magazines. From Cincinnati,
Nikki Giovanni (born 1943) publishes *Black Feeling* (1968),
a work that reveals one of the most intense and resourceful
new talents. Yet all these poets, regionally diverse, tend to
inhabit a certain area of the female sensibility, tend to write

from a certain point of view pertinent to their situation as women in the Black Movement. As Abby Lincoln puts it: "The black woman is hurt, confused, frustrated, angry, resentful, frightened *and* evil! Who in this hell dares suggest that she should be otherwise? These attitudes only point up her perception of the situation and her healthy rejection of the same."

Other poets gather in San Francisco around the *Journal of Black Poetry*, and a circle forms in New York around the magazine *Umbra*. Energetic and talented poet-anthologists, such as Larry Neal (born 1937) and Clarence Major (born 1936), author of *All Night Visitors* (1969) and *Swallow the Lake* (1970), give currency to the various movements of Black literature. It becomes evident that in still other writers —for instance, Yusef Iman and Ed Spriggs, among the more militant; Ed Bullins, better known as a dramatist, Ishmael Reed, a novelist as well; and Sun Ra and Pharaoh Saunders, musicians—the experiments of Black poetry are far from ended.

IV

DRAMA

INTRODUCTION

Of all the literary genres, the drama has the shortest and most spare tradition. Neither the Puritan inheritance nor the harsh quality of frontier life contribute to the development of a native theatre. It is not until the early part of the twentieth century that an original American drama comes into being. The dominant figure of that movement is Eugene O'Neill, who combines elements of naturalism, expressionism, and Greek tragedy in a distinctive dramatic language of great power. Throughout the Twenties and Thirties, other notable playwrights—Maxwell Anderson, Robert Sherwood, Elmer Rice, Thornton Wilder, Clifford Odets, Lillian Hellman—give diversity and magnitude to the achievement of the American theatre.

During the Forties and early Fifties, the older playwrights continue to write and stage their plays; some of O'Neill's

---

All dates after works in this section refer to first publication in book form rather than to first performance.

best work belongs to that period: *The Iceman Cometh*
(1946), *Long Day's Journey Into Night* (1956), *A Touch
of the Poet* (1957), *Hughie* (1959), *More Stately Mansions*
(1964). But the protest themes of the Thirties soon give
way to other concerns, to newer sensibilities. Thus William
Saroyan's *The Time of Your Life* (1939) and Thornton
Wilder's *The Skin of Our Teeth* (1942), though quite different, are closer to postwar drama in their use of fantasy
and free form.

In the postwar generation of playwrights, however, Tennessee Williams and Arthur Miller determine the earliest
directions of drama and dominate its stage for well over a
decade. No two dramatists can be more dissimilar. Coming
out of rural, even mythological, Mississippi, Williams plunges
into the underside of the mind, peopling his plays with violent
and exotic figures. Miller, on the other hand, comes from the
urban, Jewish milieu of New York; and though his attach-
ment to the conventions of the realistic stage weaken with
the years, he never forsakes realism as an attitude. Between
the stage production of Williams's *The Glass Menagerie* in
1944 and that of Gelber's *The Connection* and Albee's *The
Zoo Story*, both in 1959—the last two plays mark the beginning of a still newer wave in the American theatre—few
dramatists challenge the authority of Williams and Miller.
The New York theatre is given mostly to commercial plays
and musicals, productions of considerable sparkle and sophistication but seldom of enduring value. The economics of
Broadway discourages dramatic experimentation, smooths
the danger or difficulty of the individual voice. Each play
is a vastly cooperative venture; and in order to remain open,
each must become a "smash hit." Furthermore, the pressure
of other media, notably film and television, steadily mounts
on Broadway. At times, the pressure produces aesthetic adaptations of a story from one form to another; more often, the
motive of profit overrules aesthetics.

Once again, American drama begins to lag behind other genres in the first decades of the postwar era. With few exceptions, it seems enervated or derivative. The new breakthrough comes under the influence of a European movement, designated generically as the Theatre of Cruelty (Artaud) or the Theatre of the Absurd (Beckett). By the late Fifties, Williams and Miller have nearly exhausted themselves in repetition. The psychology of the former and the sociology of the latter are no longer adequate to the violence or unreason of the day; and their abstractions refer to an older conception of American culture. Meanwhile, in Europe the seminal ideas of Copeau and particularly of Artaud are rediscovered. Beckett, Brecht, Genet, and Ionesco, each unique in dramatic style, lay the foundation of a new theatre, at once dazzling and simple, and create dramatic languages of enormous possibility. A renewed interest in mime and gesture, in the space of silence, in fantasy, in simplicity, contribute to a fresh apprehension of reality.

It is a reality that postwar American writers can understand, though they choose to respond to it in ways of their own. Their dark sense of life, their intuition of the void, may not be as deep as their European compeers. Nevertheless, the new American dramatists recognize the random, contradictory, and mysterious quality of existence represented by the Theatre of the Absurd. They sense that history, politics, metaphysics are called into doubt; and that the theatre itself, as an ancient, symbolic form of the human spirit, must undergo radical transformations. Indeed, the forms of drama open, shatter; what remains on the stage is a quizzical sense of being, a poetic apprehension, beyond comedy or tragedy, perhaps beyond absurdity, of the persistence of man. As in fiction or poetry, the new drama often flourishes at the point where terror and humor, anger and celebration, nihilism and mysticism, meet.

The opportunity for developing the new American drama comes when authors, actors, and directors begin to move away from the high-rent districts of Broadway into lofts, cellars, and abandoned warehouses located in various parts of New York, mostly Greenwich Village. The economic and psychological conditions of the Off-Broadway theatre are conducive to experiment; some of the best plays of the younger dramatists—Edward Albee, Jack Gelber, Jack Richardson, Kenneth H. Brown—first see the footlights in outlying districts. But a reaction to the Off-Broadway theatre soon takes place as its iconoclasm hardens into convention. By the middle of the Sixties, an even more informal and experimental theatre, employing Happenings and Mixed Media, discovering still younger dramatists and painters and musicians, assumes the name of "OOB," Off-Off-Broadway. Small restaurants, bars, churches, and coffee houses become the scene of rehearsed or spontaneous spectacles. At times, theatrical life is the street.

New York, however, holds no monopoly on the theatre. Guerrilla Theatre, performed by student or amateur groups, hippies, yippies, or political dissenters, moves into the parks, the streets, even the courtrooms of America. At the same time, fine repertory companies, in Washington, Houston, Cleveland, Detroit, Milwaukee, Minneapolis, and San Francisco, encouraged often by grants from the Ford Foundation, produce the work of known and unknown contemporary dramatists across the country. By 1970, the prospects of American drama appear considerably more exciting than in 1950.

PROMINENT DRAMATISTS

Tennessee Williams

Thomas Lanier Williams, better known by his pen name, Tennessee Williams (born 1914), is the most prolific of postwar dramatists and perhaps the most lurid. A romantic, a solitary fantasist of desire, he can combine poetic delicacy with primal violence, capture the frailty of man's spirit and his voracity. Enacting the explosive drama of the subconscious, Williams also exposes a civilization in which deviants or outsiders, the "fugitive kind," always perish. These, however, are as often victims of their own guilt or illusion as they are prey to the world's brutality.

His vision owes something to the Southern gothic tradition, from Poe to Faulkner, and owes even more to he erotic mysteries of D. H. Lawrence, whom Williams admires. His dramatic sensationalism—his ready use of nymphomania, homosexuality, rape, castration, murder, cannibalism—which may account for his popular success, should also be seen as a projection of an imagination haunted by death. At the same time, Williams fastens on sexuality as a metaphor of life. The perversion of desire reflects the identity of his characters; its absence defines the terrors of their isolation. His ultimately religious apprehension of love prompts him to portray redemptive figures in the composite image of Christ, Orpheus, and Dionysus, who embody sacrifice, poetry, and nature in their mutilated flesh. Savage and sometimes even malignant, the dark gods promise man no pabulum, no happiness.

But drama, in Williams's view, also brings time to a stop, and thus assuages the tragedy of man. In an essay called "The Timeless World of a Play," he writes:

> About their lives people ought to remember that when they are finished, everything in them will be contained in a marvelous state of repose which is the same as that which they unconsciously admired in drama. The rush is temporary. The great and only possible dignity of man lies in his power deliberately to choose certain moral values by which to live as steadfastly as if he, too, like a character in a play were immured against the corrupting rush of time.

The arrest of time presumes a suspension of realism, and a movement into a world of poetry, dream, or terror, a world of grotesque distortions. That world the characters of Williams inhabit, though they bring to it familiar grievances, memories, names.

His first play, *Battle of Angels*, fails when it is produced in Boston in 1940, though Margaret Webster directs it and Miriam Hopkins takes the lead. Success comes some years later with *The Glass Menagerie* (1945), a vaguely autobiographical family drama, which creates in Amanda Wingfield the eternal Southern lady, steeped in genteel illusions. Amanda, living in a delicate world of fantasies, memories, and repressions, contributes to the breakdown of her crippled, inward daughter, Laura, who entombs herself in a room full of glass figurines, waiting vainly for "gentlemen callers." Laura's brother, Tom, serves as ironic narrator, both part of and apart from the action, driven at last by his own ambitions and the derangements of this familial world to flee, carrying his guilt with him. The tender beauty of the play, the mood of pervasive unhappiness, the chiaroscuro of life, wavering between real and imagined states, prevail. Symbol and theme, character and setting, act in poetic synergy to make this drama among the finest of the period.

The impact of Williams's next work, *A Streetcar Named Desire* (1947) is even greater. The element of Southern nostalgia finds more complex expression in aging Blanche DuBois, dreamy and dissolute, corrupt and spiritual, vain and self-destructive. Blanche is finally overcome by life, brutish, real, as represented by her brother-in-law, Stanley Kowalski. Even her pregnant sister, Stella Kowalski, sides in the end with her husband and her own instincts, helping to commit Blanche to a mental institution. Set in a dingy yet still exotic quarter of New Orleans, the play offers a parable of the conflicts and values of American society at midcentury, sustaining its themes with surges of dramatic vitality. More important, perhaps, the play mediates the awesome polarity of nature and civilization, fact and fancy, so central to Williams, a polarity that collapses in his later melodramatic work. Starring in its original production Jessica Tandy, Marlon Brando, and Kim Hunter, directed with flair by Elia Kazan, the play establishes a point of reference in the contemporary theatre.

Cat on a Hot Tin Roof (1955) shows Williams still possessed of his powers. Set on a Southern plantation dominated by the ruthless patriarchic figure of Big Daddy, it places in dramatic counterpoint his married descendants: Gooper and Mae, lusting after the land; and Brick and Maggie, who evade the implications of their sexual crisis. Money and sex, greed and mendacity, tear at the invisible fabric not only of a particular family or culture but also of life itself, sundered by the malice of mind and violence of instinct. In the background, hidden in the lives that Williams brilliantly reveals, human aberration or physical disease—adultery, homosexuality, alcoholism, cancer—deepen the enigma of man's moral existence.

Sometimes, Williams rewrites his earlier plays; thus *Battle of Angels* becomes *Orpheus Descending*. At other times, he expands a one-acter into a full drama; thus a short work performed at the Spoleto Festival later becomes *The Night of the Iguana*. Solitude, sexual hunger and deviation, the dread of death, always enter his most startling plays: *Summer and Smoke* (1948), *Suddenly Last Summer* (1957), *Sweet Bird of Youth* (1959), *The Milk Train Doesn't Stop Here Any More* (1963). Occasionally, redemptive elements appear in his tortured dramas: *Orpheus Descending* (1957), *The Night of the Iguana* (1961). Occasionally, also, elements of lusty comedy (*The Rose Tatoo* [1951]) or surreal comedy (*Camino Real* [1953]) or plain sex comedy (*Period of Adjustment* [1960]) relieve the aura of modernized Grand Guignol in his work. But there is no doubt that the essential

Williams believes in the "horror at the heart of the mean-
inglessness of existence"; and defines the condition of beings
"sentenced to solitary confinement" inside their own skins,
"for life."

By his own admission a rebellious Puritan, Tennessee
Williams finds the consummation of his rebellion not in sexuality but in art. His aestheticism offers an alternative to
existence: like Val Xavier, the bard of *Orpheus Descending*,
the best in Williams's world are "legless birds" who "live
their whole life on the wing" and "never light on this earth
but one time when they die." Yet Williams also takes the
full measure of American reality, and without drabness or
determinism offers major insights into its social and historic
qualities. True, he repeats himself in the theatre, employs
the clichés of melodrama, surrenders at times to pathology,
and exudes in places self-hate. But the dialogue of Williams
also echoes the morbid poetry of the age; and his characters,
supercharged with their own emotions, compel audiences to
share their fates. Above all, he expands the sensibility of
postwar drama with Orphic knowledge, however mixed.

Williams is also the author of short stories, *One Arm* (1948,
1954) and *Hard Candy* (1954); a novel, *The Roman Spring
of Mrs. Stone* (1950); poems, *In the Winter of Cities* (1956);
and a famous film script, *Baby Doll* (1956).

Arthur Miller

Unlike Williams, Arthur Miller (born 1915) has no interest
in sexual waywardness or romantic agony. He once said:
"I am tired of seeing men as merely a bundle of nerves.
That way lies pathology." A moralist foremost, endowed
with broad social awareness, Miller places an idea of commitment and responsibility at the heart of his drama. In a
long preface to his *Collected Plays* (1957) he writes: "For

I understand the symbolic meaning of a character and his career to consist of the kind of challenge he accepts and the kind he can pass by." Behind the statement lies the conviction that as life is accountable rather than absurd, so are human beings solidary, responsible in their social encounters, and creative in their discovered reverence for existence. If the individual is seldom wholly defined by his milieu, neither can he escape entirely the impersonal forces that affect his image of himself, his *name*.

At its best, Miller's dramatic vision has power, integrity. But it also retains, perhaps from the theatre of the Thirties, a certain awkward simplicity. Working in a Manhattan warehouse during the Depression, Miller sees the injustices of free enterprise, the worker's need not only for food but also for dignity. His leftist sympathies, however, do not tempt him to impose on his plays the rigid cast of ideology. Slowly, almost painfully, he tries to evolve a dramatic style, beyond realism, that can convey human transcendence, can uncover the "underlying poem of a play." In this, his greatest ambition, his success is equivocal. Still, speaking in 1972, he thus answers an interviewer: "I can't see or predict the future. But I think my plays are getting more and more mythological; the people are becoming less and less psychological."

Miller's first play, *The Man Who Had All the Luck* (1944), depicts a character who attempts to fight free of received notions of success as well as his own sense of impending disaster. The play, which runs for four performances only, fails, though it calls the attention of critics and producers to a new talent. *All My Sons* (1947) makes a wider impression. Miller implicates the domestic tragedy of Joe Keller, a war profiteer who manufactures faulty airplane engines, into larger issues of pragmatism and idealism, crime and atonement, justice and love. Technically artificial in places, and morally elusive in its final perceptions of guilt, the play indicates serious promise rather than achievement.

The achievement comes with *Death of a Salesman* (1949). This work creates the unforgettable figure of the aging Willy Loman. Moreover, it penetrates the mythology of America, whose illusions lead to Willy's ruin as salesman, husband, father, his ultimate ruin as a man. Through memory and dramatic introspection, a "mobile concurrency of past and present" retrieves his life, the bitterness and "ecstasy of spirit" that he chases to the end. The play puts not only the Lomans but a whole society on trial; above all, it questions the human condition that corrupts the need of love and reduces a bright dream to suicide. Willy fails; but his failed son, Biff, moves to redeem both father and son from their failures. That is the sole solace of a play, close at times to pathos, yet in its purposeful passion, its sobriety of scenes, undeniably a classic of postwar drama. Critical reaction to it centers on the question whether modern tragedy can be defined without reference to heroism or metaphysics. Miller himself states: "The tragic feeling is evoked in us when we are in the presence of a character who is ready to lay down his life, if need be, to secure one thing—his sense of personal dignity." Staged intensely on one versatile set by Elia Kazan, *Death of a Salesman* runs on Broadway for nearly two years.

In the early Fifties, Miller withstands the inquisition of the House Un-American Activities Committee while a wave of anti-Communist hysteria sweeps the country. From the experience comes *The Crucible* (1953). Set in Salem during the notorious witch hunts of the seventeenth century, the play presents an obvious reflection of current events, an allegory of our times. Controversy tends, therefore, to becloud its deeper interests: the inevitable clash of private and public motives, the mysterious capacity of terror to create a reality independent of fact or history, the administration of conscience. Against these, against the superstition of his neighbors, the crazed love of Abigail, the evil of his judges, John Proctor stands not so much a hero or martyr as a man possessed of full consciousness. His true enemy may be even deeper, gratuitous evil. "I think now that one of the hidden weaknesses of our whole approach to dramatic psychology is our inability . . . to conceive, in effect, of Iago," the author muses.

Increasingly, Miller is drawn, in wonderment or in horror, toward the inner sources of tragedy, the origins of human force. Thus, A View from the Bridge (1955, 1957) probes the soul of a betrayer. (The play is later expanded into two acts; in its original version, it is staged with another short piece, A Memory of Two Mondays [1955].) Eddie Carbone, a longshoreman on the Brooklyn waterfront, confused by his incestuous and homosexual lusts, caught between organized crime and economic exploitation, manages still to impose his human rage on the audience. Converted into prose from its verse original, employing a choral commentator, Alfieri, the play still tries to follow a "fine, high, always visible arc of forces."

For nine years, Miller is silent, disappointed in what he conceives to be public misunderstanding of his plays, engrossed in his own life—divorce from his first wife, marriage to and divorce from Marilyn Monroe, a third marriage. When he returns to the theatre with After the Fall (1964), he offers his most introspective and autobiographical play. A kaleidoscopic succession of scenes takes the protagonist, Quentin, in search of his past, in search of himself, beyond cruelty, egotism, and failure, to a lucid life in the shadow of despair: "Is the knowing all? To know, and even happily, that we meet unblessed; not in some garden of wax fruit and painted trees, that lie of Eden, but after, after the Fall, after many, many deaths. Is the knowing all?" Rejecting his former faith in absolutes—Socialism, Innocence, even Love—Miller traces the roots of the world's violence to the Self, and goes on to accept man's terrible complicity in the real. More mature in thought than in its rhetoric or dramaturgy, After the Fall once again fails to satisfy all the expectations that audiences rightly bring to Miller's plays.

Incident at Vichy (1965), a long one-acter, focuses its theme by narrowing the action to a Nazi hunt for Jews. But at a crucial moment in the play, the Jewish doctor, Leduc, says, "Each man has his Jew; it is the other. And the Jews have their Jews," thus turning a particular event into a withering accusation of human nature. It is to examine, and perhaps even to answer, the same accusation that Miller returns to the family situation in *The Price* (1968). Two brothers, a police sergeant and a successful doctor, face each other across sixteen years of separation, embodying two ways of life, complementary yet tragically incompatible. The play shows no real development in Miller's work, except perhaps a tough sense of the near impossibility of altruism in human relations.

Miller confronts the issues of his day with a tortured determination to shirk no truth or responsibility. He engages the world with conscience and ideas with naïve passion; he sustains the theatre with his morose art. Yet the cumulative reaction to his work remains mixed, and this, too, is understandable. For Miller seldom displays the verve, poetry, or spiritual complexity that the greatest dramatists usually command, and his imagination tends sometimes toward banality.

He is also the author of two novels, *Situation Normal* (1944) and *Focus* (1945); short stories, *I Don't Need You Any More* (1967); and a screenplay, *The Misfits* (1961), for a film starring Marilyn Monroe and Clark Gable.

Edward Albee

The most impressive of the younger dramatists who succeed Williams and Miller is Edward Albee (born 1928). His theatre is close to the style of European "absurdists"; echoes of Beckett, Genet, Ionesco, and Dürrenmatt can be heard in his plays. Still, Albee's language is entirely his own, taut or sinuously coiled, striking suddenly. The language has the force of hateful truth behind it, the force of insight into the dark twists of American culture. He understands the human drive toward self-annihilation; and likes nothing better than to expose the pretensions of familial, conjugal, and romantic love. But Albee's drama also pushes misanthropy and misogyny beyond themselves, in search of new sources of vitality. Cruelty, hatred, or spite shatter human complacencies; savage invective, absurd cliché, or gallows humor jar audiences into feeling the outrages of quotidian life. About cruelty, Albee writes: "Ever since the night I saw that great 'shoestring revue' number . . . called 'Man's Inhumanity to Man,' I've had difficulty saying it. . . . But that is what I write about. I think it's something that needs to be said." It needs to be said repeatedly since man's capacity for self-deception, in the view of Albee as of O'Neill, seems boundless. An icy moralist even more than a metaphysician, Albee denies that he partakes in destructive ceremonies for their own sake. His compassion goes out to men and women who suffer intensely without knowing how to grasp their suffering. Indeed, the development of Albee's work in a decade suggests a genuine movement toward acceptance of reality, a complex interdebtedness akin to love.

The Zoo Story (1959), rejected at first by New York producers, opens in Berlin in 1959. A year later, it is billed with Beckett's *Krapp's Last Tape* at the Off-Broadway Provincetown Playhouse, registering a macabre success. The play portrays in one wrenching scene—a simple bench in Central Park—two men, Jerry and Peter, the truculent outsider and the complacent insider, instinct against society, two sides of human nature locked in a struggle of mutual recognition, of love really, culminating in death. The single action, lashed up by Albee's language, develops into an authentic dramatic metaphor, surprising, many-faceted. The author, furthermore, discovers his own form, neither realistic nor absurd. By comparison, *The Death of Bessie Smith* (1959, 1960), which also has its premiere in Berlin, seems more conventional in its cinematic realism, its direct approach to racism in America. Yet the culprit, a Southern nurse, emerges as a human, if hysterical, character screaming: "I am tired . . . I am tired of the truth . . . and I am tired of lying about the truth . . . I am tired of my skin. . . . I WANT OUT!"

Two plays related to each other, *The Sandbox* (1959) and *The American Dream* (1960, 1961), follow. The first borrows characters from the later and longer piece, then incomplete, to create a vicious and surreal pastiche of the family. Albee describes *The American Dream* as an "attack on the substitution of artificial for real values in our society, a condemnation of complacency, cruelty, emasculation and vacuity; it is a stand against the fiction that everything in this slipping land of ours is peachy-keen." The grisly and comic action, poised at the edge of surrealism, pertains to an exiguous Daddy and cannibal Mommy in search of a handsome celluloid replica of the son she has dismembered; only Granny remains human. Cannily, Albee employs the harmless stereotypes of American life, its most cheery nonsense, to reveal the bane, sterility, or waste that Mommy calls "satisfaction."

The first full-length play of Albee, and still his best known, is *Who's Afraid of Virginia Woolf?* (1962). Four people— George and Martha, the central characters, and Nick and Honey—confront each other in every combination possible, clawing egos, stripping bodies, heaving their fears loose into the night. The drama, set in an ordinary living room of a professor's house, moves with enormous dynamism from dangerous conviviality, through fun and games and a witches' sabbath, to an exorcism that leaves the audience wholly spent in horror and recognition. Its ritual structure circles narrowly around the center; there, at the hollow center, a myth sustained by human dread of reality threatens to swallow every-thing. Exposure of the myth—it could concern God and America as well as the imaginary son of George and Martha —opens the way for harrowing reconciliation. Balanced beautifully among hateful characters and abstract contraries, singing to his music of abuse, Albee manages to imply large questions about ambivalence of human feeling, aggression and impotence between the sexes, the dialectics of cowardice and ambition in society, the collision of humanistic with scientific values, the suddenness of pity, the power of illusion.

The realm of the invisible seems to provide the aura of Albee's most ambiguous drama, *Tiny Alice* (1965). A philosophic teaser, wavering between fact and fantasy, the work presents the struggle of Brother Julian to preserve his purity and to justify his Christian faith, justify any reality untouched by human hand, in terms of his concrete existence, his suffering. Sinister and heavily allegorical, the play eludes dramatic perception; it may also elude the author's own intentions. Its obscure motifs—among them the exact maquette of a castle within an ominous castle—repel discursive knowledge. *Tiny Alice* wants to offer itself simply as a theatrical experience; but its experience mirrors the void more than anything else.

In the same period, Albee turns to adaptations from novels or plays of other writers: *The Ballad of the Sad Café* (1963), *Malcolm* (1966), *Everything in the Garden* (1968). His next original work, *A Delicate Balance* (1966), clearly shows a desire to transcend absurdity and hatred. Like *Who's Afraid of Virginia Woolf?*, the play derives its energy from domestic violence: familial contempt, solitude, madness. But its vitriolic language also purifies morality, consumes the dross of social attitudes. More than any other work of Albee, the play seeks a working concept of human responsibility, a minimal love. Its ending, almost forced in its faint hope, qualifies the insanity of man. "They say we sleep to let the

demons out," a main character says, "to let the mind go
raving mad, our dreams and nightmares all our logic gone
awry, the dark side of our reason. And when the daylight
comes again . . . comes order with it." Yet the play, mixing
its styles, reverts in part to older conventions of the Broadway theatre; and its symbolic pretensions can hardly disguise
a certain lifelessness in its characters. A later work, *Box-
Mao-Box* (1968), imitates the experimental genre of Beckett,
though its theme is too political and its style too figurative
to suit that genre.

Like Williams and Miller before him, Albee is not an
innovator in the forms of drama. At least two of his major
plays, *Who's Afraid of Virginia Woolf?* and *A Delicate Balance*, hold close to the setting, if not to the mental space,
of traditional theatre; and others reflect various European
influences. Yet there is no doubt that Albee pushes postwar
drama into new regions of sensibility. He expresses the
destructive conjunctions of human passions—love and hate,
dream and nightmare, communion and solitude—in characters, in actions, in symbols composed in ritual or musical
patterns. His vision of man's failure is darkly humorous and
so uncompromising as to possess a unique dignity. And more
than his predecessors, he denounces, in essays and interviews,
the material conditions that corrupt the art of drama in
America.

TYPES AND TRENDS
OF DRAMA

Originals and Adaptations

The original ventures of established novelists and poets in
playwriting, as well as the adaptatoins of various authors

from genres other than drama, fill a distinct vacuum in the postwar American theatre.

In *The Last Analysis* (1965) Saul Bellow writes a satire on psychoanalysis or, rather, on what he calls the "peculiarly literal and solemn manner in which Americans dedicate themselves to programs, fancies, or brainstorms." Though livened with fantastic comedy, the play fails to sustain the interest of audiences. Similarly, Joseph Heller, despite his outrageous humor, falls short of dramatic success in his play *We Bombed in New Haven* (1968). J. P. Donleavy's *Fairy Tales of New York* (1961) and John Hawkes's *The Innocent Party* (1967) hardly succeed more. Perhaps only James Purdy's short play "Cracks" (1961), a work with Beckettian overtones, comes close to fulfilling the conditions of drama.

Poets of the "New York School" also turn to drama in an attempt to create out of verse, parody, and politics a new experimental form, funny and free. John Ashbery's *The Heroes* (1960), Frank O'Hara's *Try! Try!* (1960), and Kenneth Koch's *The Election* (1960)—see also his *Bertha, and Other Plays* (1960)—are instances of their quizzical attitude toward society. The work of a different kind of poet, Lawrence Ferlinghetti's *Unfair Arguments with Existence* (1963), proves hard to produce. The outstanding poetic contribution to the theatre comes from Robert Lowell. In *The Old Glory* (1964, 1965), Lowell transforms two stories of Hawthorne, "Endicott and the Red Cross," "My Kinsman Major Molineux," and a novella of Melville, *Benito Cereno*, into a dramatic trilogy that is a troubling statement on man and history in times of revolution.

Curiously enough, adaptations very often meet the challenge of the theatre better than works intended originally for dramatic performance. Thus, for instance, Carson McCullers adapts her own novelette into a fine stage production, *The Member of the Wedding* (1950); so does Truman Capote adapt *The Grass Harp* (1952); while Albee, highly skilled as a dramatist, does only fairly with McCullers's *The Ballad of the Sad Café*, Purdy's *Malcolm*, and Giles Cooper's play, *Everything in the Garden*. Albee, nonetheless, is conscious of the difficulties of his task; he writes: "The responsibility of the playwright is double—to the work adapted and to the stage as an art form. He must sometimes alter a work radically, so that no change will seem to have taken place when it is moved from the page to the stage. He must make a work belong between curtains as much as it ever did between covers. . . . "

Understandably, the most popular adaptations of the period are from current novels: Joshua Logan's version of Thomas Heggen's *Mister Roberts* (1948), Herman Wouk's own *The Caine Mutiny* (1954), Harvey Breit and Budd Schulberg's *The Disenchanted* (1959). Television, which begins to exert its enormous influence, also contributes to the stage. Such dramas as N. Richard Nash's *The Rainmaker* (1955), Paddy Chayevsky's *Middle of the Night* (1956), Gore Vidal's *Visit to a Small Planet* (1957), and William Gibson's *The Miracle Worker* (1960) are based on television plays. But all these adaptations from popular novels or video scripts, however agreeable they may seem, contribute little to the dramatic art of the period. Sentimental in their humor, morality, or realism, they serve mainly to reassure large audiences, and confirm their expectations of life.

"Middle Drama"

By far, the greatest number of plays in the postwar period fit a strictly commercial concept of theatre. Musical comedies, lavish, raucous, and bright, dominate the "Great White Way." But a certain type of melodrama also infiltrates the neon realm. Though wide in appeal, this type exhibits more serious pretensions. Its masters are William Inge, Arthur Laurents, and Robert Anderson, who share the dubious distinction of placing the human condition in a soft focus.

William Inge (born 1913) is known for a number of plays that are still better known as Hollywood films: *Come Back, Little Sheba* (1950), *Picnic* (1953), *Bus Stop* (1955), and *The Dark at the Top of the Stairs* (1958). A Midwesterner by birth, Inge has a certain intuitive grasp of grass-roots America. He depicts common people, their loneliness, their frustrations, their muddled erotic awakenings. But his view of love tends toward superficiality, and his skillful forms rely on pathos in expression.

Arthur Laurents (born 1918) shows similar limitations in his treatment of social problems. His best play, *Home of the Brave* (1945), deals in unglamorous fashion with war in the South Pacific and anti-Semitism in America. *The Time of the Cuckoo* (1953) and especially *A Clearing in the Woods* (1957) appeal to the popular interest in psychoanalysis as a means of apprehending character and motive on the stage. But the gifts of Laurents find their happiest medium in the musical *West Side Story* (1959), which projects its social message—about youthful gang wars—through the music of Leonard Bernstein and the choreography of Jerome Robbins.

In this general category of middle drama, Robert Anderson (born 1917) wins some attention with his play, *Tea and Sympathy* (1953), about a prep-school boy accused of homosexuality. He also writes *All Summer Long* (1955) and *Silent Night, Lonely Night* (1960).

All these playwrights show a certain theatrical flair. They adhere to the old ideal of the well-made play; they also attempt to engage significant issues of their day. But their statement is finally too soft, simple, or equivocal. They flatter their audiences into a semblance of self-knowledge; and they do little to enlarge the possibilities of dramatic form. As William Gibson, "middle dramatist" of *Two for the Seesaw*

(1959) confesses: "The theatre in this country was primarily a place not in which to be serious but in which to be likeable."

Off-Broadway

The Off-Broadway theatre, especially during the Fifties, helps with new honesty and resourcefulness to remake American drama. Authors, actors, and directors of that theatre take risks; they show greater awareness of avant-garde movements in Europe; and, above all, they see the changing character of American society, challenging its values and assumptions. Dedicated to protest, they are also ingenious in their art. The trans-Atlantic devices of the Theatre of the Absurd or the Theatre of Cruelty no doubt influence them. But in their hands, absurdity takes on the hues of ideology, utopia, or gallows humor. The most talented companies performing Off-Broadway, struggling perpetually to avoid financial ruin, are The Living Theatre (founded 1951) of Julian Beck and Judith Malina, two brave and inspired artists in their own rights; and the Artists' Theatre (1953–56) of Herbert Machiz. The Circle-in-the-Square, the Phoenix Theatre, the Theater de Lys, the Cherry Lane—all located in or around Greenwich Village—are particularly hospitable to serious and experimental drama.

The turning point of the new theatre comes when *The Connection* (1960) is produced by The Living Theatre in July, 1959. The author, Jack Gelber (born 1932), conceives that work as an improvisational drama with jazz music on the theme of drug addiction, revealing a "petty and miserable microcosm" of the human condition, a universe of self-annihilation. The play owes something to the anti-form of Pirandello's *Six Characters in Search of an Author* and to the ethos of Beckett's *Waiting for Godot*, but avoids the final pessimism of both when its most lucid junkie, Solly, states:

"The man is you. . . . You are the man. You are your own connection. It starts and stops here." By playing on the double sense of the title word, by refusing to cast the junkie simply as an outsider who must be rehabilitated into society, Gelber shows that he wants to resist pathology as much as determinism. Also, by blurring the distinction between actors and audiences—some of the former circulate during intermission, soliciting money for a quick fix—Gelber mocks the conventions of his art, and challenges everyone—author, actor, director, spectator—to take responsibility for his life, to begin his salvation. *The Connection* proves highly controversial because its shape, its subject, its obscene language, jar the deadened sensibilities of the day; even the critics, with the notable exceptions of Harold Clurman and Kenneth Tynan, sadly miss its import. But the play finally establishes itself in the new repertory thanks to the tenacity of its producers. It is therefore all the more unfortunate that Gelber's next work, *The Apple* (1960), fails to enhance his achievement. The play, which requires actors to use their real names, possesses a zany theatrical violence, an absurd joy of life; its author seems intent on blasting every kind of bigotry and cowardice. But the impact of its hackneyed horseplay hardly equals Gelber's intention: his hope of opening wide the gates of awareness. Nor does *Square in the Eye* (1966) surpass in quality or complexity his first play.

Subsequent directions of the Off-Broadway theatre are various and its authors eclectic. Murray Schisgal (born 1926), for instance, finds English producers more receptive to his earliest efforts, two one-act plays called *The Typists and The Tiger* (1963), staged in London in 1960 and three years later in America. Gifted in dialogue, both satiric and compassionate, Schisgal perceives the waste and rage of treadmill lives in humorous terms. With more wit than originality —the twists of Ionesco's plots and syntax can be sometimes glimpsed in his plays—he tries to adapt caricature and burlesque to a deft dramatic style. He reaches Broadway with *Luv* (1965), which owes its great success more to the brilliant direction of Mike Nichols than to its own profundity. On Broadway, as in *Jimmy Shine* (1969), or off, as in *Fragments, Windows, and Other Plays* (1965), Schisgal fails to create the authentic new statement that his first work intimates.

A more subtle and probing mind, Jack Richardson (born 1935) does not achieve the wide reputation he fully deserves. His first play, *The Prodigal* (1960), retells the myth of Orestes, pitting original conceptions of Agamemnon and Aegisthus against one another, raising fundamental questions about history, morality, and dream. Limpid in its style and classic in its patterns of dramatic confrontations—the French tradition from Gide to Giraudoux comes to mind—the work, nevertheless, strikes at the center of contemporary chaos. *Gallows Humor* (1961) claims "tragicomedy" as its mode. In a preface, its author explains: "Comedy, on its highest level, has exactly the same kernel as its opposite—namely, the celebrated tragic flaw." The drama develops two moments in the lives of a condemned man and of his executioner. The two moments of freedom throw into relief the institutional death that prevails under the semblance of social order. Thus, Richardson gives dignity and reference to the term "gallows humor," so often used by superficial writers in their avoidance of pain. His dramas of ideas—a later ambitious play called *Lorenzo* fails on Broadway in 1962—are sometimes static; yet he remains among the very few to engage major themes.

Among these few, Kenneth H. Brown (born 1936) makes a lasting impression with his play, *The Brig*, published in the *Tulane Drama Review* (Spring, 1964). Set in a Marine stockade, with barbed wire and cage-like cells as part of its decor, the drama relies on harsh noise and gesture, ritual and explosive action, to enhance an atmosphere of terror, monotony, and utter degradation. Without characters—the prisoners are mere numbers—or narrative line, *The Brig* offers itself as an almost unbearable experience of absolute and arbitrary authority, of human madness as will to power. It is, in fact, as the author says, an "indictment of the senses in order to reach the soul." Its kinship to Artaud's concepts of a sensuous and cruel theatre is clear. Yet in the original production of The Living Theatre, full of actor improvisations, it is also clear that Brown has gone farther, creating a dramatic symbol outside of verbal discourse, beyond naturalism or surrealism, based on the ancient, the unacknowledged, dread of his audience. The symbol emerges from a visceral experiment unique among American playwrights. Brown's following work, however, *Three Dreams from Dell's Couch* (unpublished), which represents dreams on a special raised stage, does not impress the critics.

In a lighter, whackier mood, Arthur Kopit (born 1937) writes plays full of frippery, parody, and acrid black humor. *Oh Dad, Poor Dad, Mamma's Hung You in the Closet and I'm Feelin' So Sad* (1960), directed with bravura by Jerome Robbins, suggests in its very title the macabre sex and absurdism of its genre; a growing Venus flytrap, a talking piranha, sliding chairs and banging doors are part of its set. But Kopit's comic gift—elements of the Marx Brothers and of pseudo-Harlequin are in it—seems finally too facile, a witty evasion, Camp. Still young as a dramatist, his future development is hard to foretell. A later work, *Indians* (1969) —about myths and facts of the West, capitalism and primitivism, pioneers and Indians, all contradictions embodied hilariously, sadly, in the person of Buffalo Bill—shows new skill and seriousness.

There are, of course, other dramatists of the Off-Broadway theatre: William Hanley, Arnold Weinstein, William Snyder, Jules Feiffer, among others. Clearly, no single direction, no uniformity of theme or method, prevails in that theatre. It produces such signal works as Gelber's *The Connection,*

Albee's *The Zoo Story*, and Brown's *The Brig*; it welcomes the admirable, and rather classic plays of Richardson; and it presents the extravaganzas of Schisgal and Kopit.

Off-Off-Broadway

Inevitably, as some dramatists of the Off-Broadway theatre achieve renown, they begin to turn to the financial rewards of larger media. Inevitably, too, the Off-Broadway theatre gradually surrenders to commercialization as its audiences and advertisements spread wider. A time comes for a more reckless or untrammeled drama. Thus the Off-Off-Broadway theatre comes into being.

Again, the still newer theatre has no manifesto or monolithic character. It appears as an improvised or casual community theatre as well as an avant-garde training ground. Its main resource is human talent, energy, commitment. At times, it seems exceedingly cultist, thespian parties, jokes of a clique. More often, it asserts its freedom from public acceptance and economic gain in highly imaginative terms. With such liberty, the distinction between amateurs and professionals tends to vanish; the actors take odd jobs to support themselves, and the line between audience and actors becomes harder to discern.

The arbitrary beginning may be a performance of Jarry's *King Ubu* at a Greenwich Village coffeehouse called Take 3, in September, 1960. Soon, the practice spreads to other locations, particularly active on Monday nights when Off-Broadway is dark, though civic rulings and licensing problems nearly cripple these efforts. The most notable centers of the new theatre are Joseph Cino's The Caffé Cino; the Judson Poets' Theatre, organized by Al Carmines, assistant minister of the Judson Memorial Church, where many of the performances take place; Ellen Stewart's resourceful La Mama

Experimental Theatre Club; Theatre Genesis, run by Ralph Cook, lay minister of St. Mark's In The Bowery Church; and Joseph Chaikin's The Open Theatre, which includes some of the most active participants in Off-Off-Broadway. Other groups include The American Theatre for Poets, the Hardware Poet's Playhouse, and the Albee-Barr-Wilder Playwright's Unit.

In style, Off-Off-Broadway favors short and striking plays, several of which can be presented in an evening. Rarely naturalistic, it is comic in devious and disturbing ways, and consummately American in violence or extravagance. Though its artistic and political tempers are mainly radical, it avoids direct statement, preachment, ideology. As Joseph Chaikin puts it: "We are trying to use the theatre to make visible the human situation at a time when 'things could be different.' But only some of the work and thought is in social terms. Much of the work is abstract and nonliteral." Above all, drama employs the resources of a "total theatre": mixed media, technological devices, physical shock and improvisation, a language even less restricted to words than European dramas of the absurd. But the main ingredients, as Ellen Stewart puts it, are "warm bodies, bare boards, imagination, and lots of youth and energy." At times, the theatre expresses a sense of apocalyptic urgency as well as a hope for human community. Ralph Cook, for instance, says: "Personally I have little hope for the survival of our civilization. But whatever hope we have lies with our artists, for they alone have the ability . . . to withstand the onslaught of the mass media and the multitudes of false gods. . . . Within this instantaneous electronic age the world is rapidly becoming one tribe, and the artist is assuming his original role of tribal actor and artificer." Underlying the effort is a certain faith that Al Carmines articulates thus: " . . . believing in people, we also believe in the validity of the theatrical event—and that's what keeps us going." A theatre of this kind is particularly difficult to review or explain in discursive language.

Though a great many playwrights contribute to Off-Off-Broadway, several are particularly known for their flair and stamina in the genre. Paul Foster (born 1931) has a small international following. His plays, *Hurrah for the Bridge* (1964) and *Tom Paine* (1968), performed at La Mama, display unusual dexterity in mixing media and techniques. In *Balls* (1964), Foster holds the stage only with two Ping-Pong balls swinging in the void while a tape carries sounds from the sea, and hypnotic voices weave pleasure, pain, determination, protest, fear, through time and eternity. No actors appear in this disquieting drama, which echoes Beckett from afar.

Jean-Claude Van Itallie (born 1935) produces his plays both in America and abroad. He is best known, perhaps, for *America Hurrah* (1966), which uses horrendous dolls, larger than life-size, to deride the vulgarity and violence, the bloated quality, of culture in the United States. Noise, glare, caricature, and grotesquerie—obscene drawings, too—carry the coarse point to the audience. His other plays include *War* (1967) and *Serpent* (1969).

Young and prolific, Sam Shepard (born 1943) writes plays for Off-Off-Broadway characterized by a special subjective vitality and a highly visual sense of drama. In *Chicago* (1965), no narrative or logical thread relates the action; a young man speaks from a bathtub while various characters, with suitcases and fishing poles, cross the stage. Stu, the young man, utters his disjointed and funny monologues in various styles, offering a slanting critique of life. A longer work, *La Turista* (1968), moves from one parodic mode to another in absurd tableaux full of unstated violence, composing an ineluctable statement on the psychic disease of man.

There are, of course, many other authors—Frank O'Hara, Lanford Wilson, Joel Oppenheimer, Megan Terry, Ronald

Tavel, Maria Irene Fornes, Rosalyn Drexler—who contribute
to the diversity of Off-Off-Broadway. There are also painters,
dancers, sculptors, and musicians who help to broaden the
conception of theatrical events. These are called Happenings
ever since Allan Kaprow, a pop painter, staged *18 Happenings in 6 Parts*, at the Reuben Gallery on October 4, 1959.

Happenings are sometimes meticulously planned, sometimes full of surprise and improvisation. Almost always, they
encourage audience participation, thus implicating "art"
wholly into "life." They also engage several media simultaneously, turning the environment into an active sensorium.
Process, diversity, and surprise prevail over verbal statement,
and discontinuity shapes the form. At their best, Happenings
aim at more than entertainment; they try to alter consciousness, perception. The lessons of Dada have been learned by
authors of the genre. But more immediately, perhaps, the
works of composers Marcel Duchamp and of John Cage—
the latter directs an ur-happening at Black Mountain College
in 1952—influence them. Duchamp's mystic geometry of
found objects and Cage's sacramental concern with randomness and Zen open new doors. Besides Kaprow, a number
of famous artists—such as Red Grooms, Robert Whitman,
Jim Dine, Claes Oldenburg, Andy Warhol—evolve diverse
kinds of Happenings. Within their various styles, some pure
intuition of action or play struggles outward. It is an intuition that no European movement, not even Surrealism, expresses in quite the same form. Perhaps the panache of
Off-Off-Broadway drama finally owes something to that
sense of play.

Black Drama

Black drama thrives on and off Broadway; it gains its
identity from its particular concerns. Committed to a racial
cause, it seldom permits itself the luxury of absurdist phi-

losophy or sheer entertainment. Its themes are, often violently, cultural; its forms vary from ritual to propaganda, from magic to fantasies of revenge. What it loses in universality, it attempts to recover in Black consciousness, Negritude. Holding some uneasy region between art and politics, it challenges the canons of Western aesthetics, but does not always succeed in formulating a theory of its own. Within its expanding domain, it evinces different styles, attitudes.

James Baldwin (born 1924), better known as a novelist and essayist, also writes plays. Like many Black authors, he increasingly finds the "war between his social and artistic responsibilities all but irreconcilable." He knows that all protest is not literature; but he also knows that no Negro can escape his past, "blood dripping down through the leaves. . . . " *The Amen Corner* (1968), written fifteen years before its publication, reflects his early interest in religious and domestic conflicts. The oppressive Christianity of the play thwarts happiness, excuses pain; it is through renewed love of her family that the protagonist, Sister Margaret, rediscovers the Lord. Weighed down by its realistic clichés, *The Amen Corner*, nonetheless, defines its own experience, unobsessed with "Whitey." A later work shows how much Black anger has developed in less than a decade. *Blues for Mister Charlie* (1964), dedicated to Medgar Evers, a civil rights worker murdered in 1963 in Mississippi, presents a vaguely similar incident in which the white killers remain defiantly free. Set in "Plaguetown, U.S.A.," the play echoes some themes from Camus's novel *The Plague*. Awkward or sentimental in parts, Baldwin's drama still manages to create an effect more complex than stark political protest. It refuses to surrender itself to hate; resists the power of evil in Self as in Other; and perceives, perhaps too briefly, the ambiguities of immolation. Judging Baldwin as a playwright, however, few critics can ascribe to him mastery or invention of dramatic forms.

Lorraine Hansberry (1930–1965) has wider success with smooth plays. She dies before the Black movement hits its shrillest note; her dramas recognize the universality of suffering even when fury and frustration threaten to overwhelm their characters. *A Raisin in the Sun* (1959), set in the Chicago Southside, elicits the matriarchic resentments and the self-hatred of which a desperate minority is capable even in its quest for dignity. Presented as a naturalistic family drama, it also catches the peculiar contradictions of the American Negro in contrast with his African brother. *The Sign in Sidney Brustein's Window* (1965) exposes those failures of white liberalism—piety, self-deception, ease of commitment—that militant Blacks condemn. Here, however, the Brusteins stand as examples of conscience hindered by irresponsibility, innocence tainted by indolence or indifference. The weaknesses they exhibit are not merely personal; they are the difficulties of commitment—for Black or White alike—in a world both savage and ambiguous. Her best play, *Les Blancs*, was produced posthumously, in 1970. Set in a medical mission in the heart of Africa—very much like Albert Schweitzer's at Lambaréné—it explores the large issues of colonialism, Christianity, and revolution with firm insight, and with theatricality equal to its compassion. An enemy of nihilism and despair, Lorraine Hansberry also opposes absurdism in literature. She parodies Albee in *The Sign in Sidney Brustein's Window* and answers Genet's *Les Nègres* in her last play. She writes: "In spite of some awe-inspiring talents involved in recent writing, the appointment of sinister universality to Ego in settings of timeless torture has been a virtual abdication of the meaning of history. . . . " But her own meliorism does not always evade the pieties of which she accuses liberals; nor does her dramatic vision always transcend the soft rhetoric of her characters.

At the other pole of Black drama, Imamu Amiri Baraka, formerly LeRoi Jones (born 1934), uses the theatre mainly as a political weapon, an extension of Black Power. To him, the theatre is not a medium of "protest," which Blacks see as a concession to the White world; it is rather an expression of Black culture, a mode of self-consciousness as well as of assault. Baraka's Revolutionary Theatre has only superficial resemblances to the Theatre of Cruelty of Artaud or Genet, which still adheres to formal art. Direct in its hatred, impatient with the obliqueness of drama, abusive and at times hysterical, the Revolutionary Theatre tends to draw energy from the passion of its audience rather than the imagination of its author. At its best, however, it draws also on the poetry, music, dance, on all the iconographies of Black culture. In 1964, Baraka organizes the Black Arts Repertory Theatre School in Harlem; and later, he founds Spirit House, a community theatre in Newark. He says: "Our theatre will show victims so that their brothers in the audience will be better able to understand that they are the brothers of victims, and that they themselves are blood brothers. . . . We will scream and cry, murder, run through the streets in agony, if it means some soul will be moved, moved to actual life understanding of what the world is, and what it could be." To his own dramatic words, Baraka brings intense poetry and rage. His first play, the one-act *The Toilet* (1963), a homosexual fantasy of politics and violence set in a public urinal, serves only to presage his obsessions. *Dutchman* (1964), however, is a dramatic masterpiece. The action between a White woman, Lula (or Eve), and a Black man, Clay (or Adam), takes place in a subway car—the symbolic "flying underbelly of the city," perhaps of existence. The action moves with truth, ferocity, and surprise toward a climax that contains the racial history of America. Within the play's brief span, language and character have the clarity that comes from deep agony; however particular, the situation renders a hellish vision of all life. *The Slave* (1964), set against an apocalyptic background of racial strife, lacks tension because its dramatic situation seems so starkly, so murderously one-sided. But in *Slaveship* (1967) Baraka resorts to a series of tableaux, a historical pageant of the Negro, a kind of "total theatre" that, although partial in its ideology, deploys in its "metalanguage" an experience larger than any of its verbal parts.

Another dramatist, extreme in his political ideas as he is artistically gifted, Ed Bullins (born 1935) brings to the theatre great energy and a special feeling for the Black experience, which he shows to be savage, funny, obscene, structureless, twisted by oppression, and robbed of a future. Several of his plays—including *How Do You Do?* (1967), and *Clara's Old Man, Goin' a Buffalo, In the Wine Time, A Son Come Home,* and *The Electronic Nigger,* collected in *Five Plays* (1969)—are staged between 1965 and 1968. As a resident playwright and associate director of the New Lafayette Theatre in Harlem, and as an editor of *Black Theatre,* his influence is considerable. His work, *The Duplex* (1972), is also produced at Lincoln Center.

Black drama continues to find new paths through authors still relatively unknown: Adrienne Kennedy, Ron Milner, Julian Mayfield, Ben Caldwell, Yusef Iman, Jimmy Garrett, among others. And Black community theatres spread from New York—westward across the United States to California, eastward to Africa. In New York, particularly, the productions of the Negro Ensemble Company—founded by Douglas Turner Ward, himself a playwright, Robert Hooks, and Gerald Krone, and supported by the Ford Foundation—proves of special distinction.

V

WITHOUT CONCLUSION

There may have been a time when literary historians could feel secure toward authors simply because these were situated in the past; such authors knew their place. But this time is over. History now seems to rest on quicksand, and its invisible reaches are structures of our own intellects. Nor is the literary text itself considered, as it once was, an immutable statement, transmitting its true meaning through the years. More often, the text is perceived through the kaleidoscope of our consciousness, a changing and many-colored thing.

If these difficulties attend the literary historian, how much more do they affect the critic of contemporary literature! The temptation of such a critic may be to play a vatic role, and thus actively to participate in the enterprise of the literary imagination. The difficulties attending that role are even greater. In the end, the critic can do only what any reader of current literature must also do: accept both the tact and willfulness of his reading as a provisional measure of his life in this time and this place.

A reader of contemporary American literature may sometimes wonder how long art or man will endure. These are radical questions that concern the very nature of being, questions that the American imagination has never ceased to pursue. Yet such queries, bouncing off the limits of the possible, return in another shape. The same reader will also note that contemporary literature seeks to reaffirm human existence in what may be termed a post-humanist future; and that in the putative death of art, the imagination discovers for itself a new domain.

Setting aside these ultimate questions, however, we may still want to ask: What will the concrete forms of literary innovation be in the Seventies? It is always possible that few innovations will take place. Rapid change is exacerbating, and a mood of cultural conservatism in the early part of the decade may favor classicism or restraint. This is sometimes implied in the anguished wit of editorials appearing in *The New York Times Book Review*. But reaction can do no more than veil the direction of real change. It is more probable that the hybrid forms of the late Sixties will continue to evolve, and that in fiction, poetry, drama, essay, and criticism still other experiments will re-create our expectations of literature. New media and new technologies may have a lasting impact on the dispositions of the imagination in culture. A Blakean marriage between mythology and technology, between the natural inheritance of man and his self-made powers of change, may even occur.

The experimental urge in fiction appears in certain younger novelists who begin to establish themselves in the Seventies. This urge manifests itself strongly in fantasy and humor, in surreal language and narrative discontinuity, and sometimes in typographic play. Within this general area of sensibility —prefigured by William Gaddis in his remarkable thousand-page-long novel, *The Recognitions* (1955), prefigured also by the fiction of Heller, Barth, Pynchon, and Barthelme— considerable variations of theme, style, and literary intent may be observed.

The most laconic of these new writers, Richard Brautigan (born 1934) is perhaps best known for *A Confederate General from Big Sur* (1964), *Trout Fishing in America* (1967), and *In Watermelon Sugar* (1968), as well as for his poetry. Lucid, precise, whimsical, idyllic, Brautigan develops a unique fragmentary style: his "chapters" are sometimes no longer than his chapter headings. Yet beneath the surface of happy love and naïve humor, the reader feels the lurking presence of loss, madness, death, feels some great blankness enfolding the rivers and wrecking yards of Brautigan's America. Mocking the conventions of fiction, Brautigan engages both silence and speech in his rigorous art, spare as a haiku. A Californian, he has some affinities with the Zen sweetness of Snyder and Kerouac; but his knowledge of the dark also recalls Hemingway.

Ronald Sukenick (born 1932), author of *Up* (1968), *The Death of the Novel, and Other Stories* (1969), and *Out* (1973), is a gifted experimental writer. He improvises himself even as he invents his characters, redefining both fact and dream. Mainly, he wants to dissolve rigid structures of human identity, artistic fable, and prose paragraph. A devotee of Wallace Stevens, Sukenick understands how the supreme fictions of the mind constantly remake the forms of reality. About the novel form, specifically, Sukenick says: "Nobody is willing to suspend disbelief in that particular way anymore, including me. So once you get to the point where you admit that you are writing a book and it *is* a book, there really is no difference between fantasy and realistic action. It's completely continuous—it's all made up."

Already prolific, Jerome Charyn (born 1937) writes several works of fiction, including *Going to Jerusalem* (1967), which

mirrors grotesquely the grotesqueness of contemporary culture; *American Scrapbook* (1969), about a Nisei internment
camp; and *Eisenhower, My Eisenhower* (1971), a wild and
chilling fantasy of America. Although Charyn does not experiment radically with the novel form, he brings to it great
verve and inventiveness, and a sense of hyperbolic humor.
His special gift is a bizarre style that renders with ferocity
the sad social facts of our time.

A brilliant novelist searching the mysteries of time and
identity, Charles Newman (born 1938) writes *New Axis*
(1966) and *The Promisekeeper* (1971). "Fiction exists in
time in a double sense," he says. "It tells us how we live—
and how we choose to speak about it. . . . The former is
usually associated with linear realism, with history; the latter
with experimentalism, linguistics. . . . The novelist ignores
this easy compartmentalization; his privilege is to bind these
senses. . . . " In his first work, Newman tells what it means
to grow up in a changing America, tells it with crisp and
consummate art. In his second and more venturesome work,
he exposes the exhaustion of two related styles, one of life,
the other of art: melioristic liberalism and didactic fiction.
The novel sets voices and visions at play, fragments of life
seeking final reconstitution. Newman also edits the distinguished literary magazine *TriQuarterly*.

"Patarealism," a term coined by Ishmael Reed (born 1938),
aptly describes the extravagant absurdities of his two novels,
The Free-Lance Pall Bearers (1967) and *Yellow Back Radio
Broke Down* (1969). Terror, laughter, and anarchy strike in
Reed's imagination, which draws on Black experience—
phrases like "crazy dada nigger" occur in his work—yet
refuses the definitions of any society. Elements of madcap
violence, hip argot, tall tale, pornography, and "Hoo-Doo"
—Reed's version of African juju magic—abound in his fiction.
As for the novel form itself, a character says: "It can be any-

thing it wants to be, a vaudeville show, the six o'clock news, the mumblings of wild men saddled by demons."

Rudolph Wurlitzer (born 19??) is an oneiric novelist, a geomancer of the dark regions, Beckettian in his incantatory silences. *Nog* (1969), subtitled a "headventure," takes us through outer America—a land of nocturnal figures, Indians, desert rats, acid heads—on the wings of the narrator's poetic madness. *Flats* (1970) goes farther in making language and consciousness almost purely spatial. People, pronouns, and places exchange their names, their identity. The sounds of words—Memphis, Omaha, Flagstaff, and so on across the nation—signify various states of futile awareness, states trying to coexist in the same mental space. As in Beckett's *Watt* or *How It Is*, entity supplants entity, voice blends into voice, fictions unwind, nothing happens. Controlled maniacally, the language of Wurlitzer forces the novel to turn back upon itself, without distractions.

Both Joyce and Beckett seem to inspire the scintillant language and self-parodic intent of Robert Coover (born 1932). In *The Universal Baseball Association, Inc.* (1968) Coover creates a rich fictional world within a fiction that ends by casting a shadow on the novelist's role. The baseball fantasies of an accountant called J. Henry Waugh also become a microcosm of American reality, indeed, of existence; the exhaustive illusions of one man warn against the exhaustion of human destiny. Coover's imagination is even more riotous in the stories of *Pricksongs and Descants* (1969). Contrapuntal in their structure as in their themes of horror and wit, death and love, these stories dislocate time, space, and causality. Above all, they consciously dramatize the self-consciousness of the author, reflecting both his difficulty as fabulist and his success as creator of "new modes of attention."

Obviously, these novelists do not make a school. Nor are they all committed to some abstract hypothesis concerning the "death of the novel." They are, however, all determined to reconceive fiction—the very nature of language and narrative—in terms more adequate to crucial changes in American culture and consciousness.

Similarly, no single experimental school dominates poetry. Pop lyrics, we know, create a fervent following, especially among the young. Since the performances of Chuck Berry in the late Fifties, these lyrics are sung to new and sophisticated sounds compounded of rock, country, blues, gospels, and folk music; and their high moment comes, in 1969, in such festivals as Woodstock and Altamont. The original talents of Bob Dylan, John Lennon and Paul McCartney, Leonard Cohen, and Jacques Brel suggest the international scope of a genre that goes farther than open-form poetry in challenging academic assumptions.

Among American poets of rock, Bob Dylan (born 1941) in particular possesses unique technical skills that serve his complex and constantly evolving vision of life. Dylan's songs, in such albums as *Bob Dylan* (1961), *Bringing It All Back Home* (1965), *Blonde on Blonde* (1966), *John Wesley Harding* (1968), and *New Morning* (1970), go to the very private center in which politics and religion, love and solitude, history and death, ecstasy and banality all meet.

Yet few literary critics concern themselves with Dylan or with the impact of pop lyrics generally on the poetic sensibility of the age. Some anthologies, such as Richard Goldstein's *The Poetry of Rock* (1969) and John Schmittroth and John Mahoney's *New Poets New Music* (1970), attempt to capture the peculiar power of the genre in print. This is difficult; for the new rock minstrels greatly depend on voice and music, on presence. At once sly and apocalyptic, cool and outrageous, studied and improvisational, they also adapt current technologies to their ancient bardic role. As Allan Ginsberg puts it: "Dylan and Donovan and some fragments of the Rolling Stones because they *think* not only in words but also in music simultaneously have out of the necessities of their own space-age media and electric machinery tunes evolved a natural use of—a personal realistic imaginative rhymed verse."

Concrete poetry differs sharply from pop lyrics both in the nature and breadth of its appeal. Ingenious, witty, eye-pleasing, concrete poetry assumes that words can plastically create or imitate their meanings; a poem's printed form contains its sense. Although several kinds of concrete poetry develop, the fundamental requirement of all, according to Mary Ellen Solt, is "concentration upon the physical material from which the poem or text is made." Thus language is reduced to pure lines or sounds or kinetic sequences; and its semantic function is remade into another aesthetic medium prefigured by the typographic experiments of Stéphane Mallarmé, Guillaume Apollinaire, Ezra Pound, and E. E. Cummings. In the postwar era, however, it is a Swiss, Eugen Gomringer, and three Brazilians, Haroldo and Augusto de Campos and Décio Pignatari, who give concrete poetry a specific identity.

Contemporary practitioners of the genre in America are Mary Ellen Solt (born 1920), editor of *Concrete Poetry: A World View* (1968) and author of *The Peoplemover* (1970); Emmett Williams (born 1925), author of *The Last French-fried Potato* (1967) and editor of *An Anthology of Concrete Poetry* (1967); and Jonathan Williams (born 1929), author of *The Lucidities* (1967) and *An Ear in Bartram's Tree* (1969). Others, younger still, include Vito Hannibal Acconci, who experiments ruthlessly with mixed media; and Aram Saroyan, Richard Kostelanetz, Robert Lax, Dick Higgins, and Ronald Johnson.

But the future of American verse will probably include more than rock and concrete poetry. Leafing through some anthologies of recent verse—Paul Carroll's *The Young American Poets* (1968) or Geof Hewitt's *Quickly Aging Here:*

Some Poets of the 1970's (1969)—one senses an excitement still undefined by the terminologies of criticism. Certainly the diverse qualities of Louise Glück and Diane Wakoski, Charles Simic and Mark Strand, indicate no prevalent school or style. And there are still other poets not mentioned in these anthologies—Ed Sanders, John Haines, Keith Waldrop, Michael Anania, John Matthias—who give various promise to the experimental strain in poetry.

In theatre, several new companies are active in discovering young playwrights and in performing experimental works. The Public Theater of Joseph Papp, who begins by directing Shakespearean plays in Central Park, is particularly vital. In the last few years, Papp stages work by Black dramatists —Sonia Sanchez, Neil Harris, Oyamo and Ilunga Adell—and also by White dramatists—Murray Mednick, John Ford Noonan, and Jason Miller.

The Performance Group of Richard Schechner thrives on controversy. One of its more sensational productions, *Dionysus in 69*, is an adaptation of *The Bacchae* by Euripides. The play expresses the new body consciousness as well as sexual violence on stage. But its theme is also political. As Schechner puts it: "Liberty can be swiftly transformed into its opposite, and not only by those who have a stake in reactionary government."

Three other organizations conceive themselves mainly as a playwright's theatre. The American Place Theatre of Wynn Handman has a special Writers Development Program that sponsors authors as different as Robert Lowell, Anne Sexton, Ed Bullins, and George Tabori. Although it makes a deliberate effort to increase the heterogeneity of audiences, the American Place Theatre also permits new dramatists to choose their directors and to produce their plays without any audiences whatever.

The Chelsea Theater Center of Robert Kalfin, subsidized by the Brooklyn Academy of Music, produces strong plays by relatively unknown talents. Its policy is to rearrange completely the space in its auditorium to suit each play. Over the years, it stages work by Imamu Amiri Baraka (LeRoi Jones), John Hawkes, and William Golding, as well as work by such newcomers as Edward Bond, Heathcote Williams, Archie Shepp, Gary Munn, Gordon Porterfield, and Joe McCord.

The New Theatre Workshop of Stephen Aaron also attempts to create for each dramatist an environment that enables him to realize the potentials of his craft. "A writer is accepted into our workshop only on the basis of several plays; at first we are more interested in the writer than in any particular script at hand," Aaron says. Once chosen, the play is first given a staged reading. Eventually, the work appears, without scenery, in the Monday Night Play Series on four successive weeks.

What these organizations have in common is a genuine concern for new playwrights, and for dramatic works that neither Broadway nor Off-Broadway theatres may find economical to produce. Scattered across New York, they derive their character not from a geographical location but from the personal force of their gifted directors.

Yet no theatre, however skillfully directed, can flourish without original playwrights. Some of the best dramatists of the Seventies are Black; they find in the oral, communal, and rhythmic or ritualistic forms of the theatre the fullest expression of their talents. But there are at least two new white playwrites who deserve special notice: David Rabe (born 19??) and Michael Weller (born 1942). Rabe's two plays, *Sticks and Bones*, and *The Basic Training of Pavlo Hummel*, strikingly portray the impact of the Vietnam war on American society. Both works are produced in 1971–72 at the Public Theater. Weller's *Moonchildren* appears first in London's Royal Court Theatre and in Washington's Arena Stage in 1968; four years later, it runs briefly on Broadway.

The play is a virtuoso verbal performance, jubilant and penetrating in its depiction of American youth, of life, really, under the aspect of its quizzical presence.

These are only a few of the names and trends that may assert themselves in the Seventies. Other names and other trends may eventually prove more central. Yet one thing is certain: that contemporary American literature takes the full measure of life in the contemporary world. Whatever mutations of artistic language or brute reality we may experience in future decades, we may be satisfied that the American imagination has been neither paltry nor laggard. And still it seeks to make our world habitable and newly human. Everything suffers a sea-change or space-change.

BIBLIOGRAPHY

Bibliographies, Dictionaries, Encyclopedias

Blanck, Jacob Nathaniel. *Bibliography of American Literature.* 5 vols. to date. New Haven: Yale University Press, 1955–69.

Cambridge History of American Literature. William Trent et al., eds. 3 vols. New York: G. P. Putnam's Sons, 1917–21.

Contemporary Authors. Clare D. Kinsman and Mary Ann Tennenhouse, eds. 32 vols. to date. Detroit, Mich.: Gale Research Co., 1962–present.

Ghodes, Clarence. *Bibliographical Guide to the Study of the Literature of the U. S. A.* 2nd ed. Durham, N. C.: Duke University Press, 1963.

Hart, James D. *The Oxford Companion to American Literature.* 4th ed. New York: Oxford University Press, 1965.

Herzberg, Max John, ed. *The Reader's Encyclopedia of American Literature.* New York: Crowell, 1962.

Jones, Howard Mumford, and Richard M. Ludwig, eds. *Guide to American Literature and Its Backgrounds since 1890.* 3rd ed. Cambridge, Mass.: Harvard University Press, 1964.

Kunitz, Stanley J. and Howard Haycraft. *Twentieth Century Authors.* New York: H. W. Wilson, 1942.

Leary, Lewis. *Articles on American Literature, 1900–1950.* Durham, N. C.: Duke University Press, 1954.
————. *Articles on American Literature, 1950–1967.* Durham, N. C.: Duke University Press, 1970.
Leary, Lewis, ed. *Contemporary Literary Scholarship: A Critical Review.* New York: Appleton-Century-Crofts, 1958.
Nilon, Charles H. *Bibliography of Bibliographies in American Literature.* New York: R. R. Bowker, 1970.
PMLA. Supplement. Annual Bibliographies. New York, 1923–present.

General Surveys

Cunliffe, Marcus. *The Literature of the United States.* Baltimore: Penguin Books, 1954.
Quinn, Arthur Hobson et al. *The Literature of the American People: An Historical and Critical Survey.* New York: Appleton-Century-Crofts, 1951.
Spiller, Robert E. *The Cycle of American Literature.* 3rd ed. New York: The Free Press, 1967.
Spiller, Robert E., et. al., eds. *Literary History of the United States.* 2 vols. 3rd ed. New York: Macmillan, 1963. Note Bibliographical Supplement.
Taylor, Walter Fuller. *The Story of American Letters.* rev. ed. Chicago: Regnery Press, 1956.

Outlines of Twentieth-Century Literature

Heiney, Donald. *Recent American Literature.* Great Neck, N. Y.: Barron, 1958.
Kostelanetz, Richard, ed. *The New American Arts.* New York: Collier, 1967.
Millett, Fred B. *Contemporary American Authors: A Critical Survey and Bio-Bibliography.* New York: Harcourt, 1940.
Spiller, Robert E., ed. *A Time of Harvest: American Literature, 1910–1960.* New York: Hill & Wang, 1962.

Straumann, Heinrich. *American Literature in the Twentieth Century.* 3rd ed. New York: Harper & Row, 1965.

Thorp, Willard. *American Writing in the Twentieth Century.* Cambridge: Harvard University Press, 1960.

Contemporary Fiction

Aldridge, John W. *After the Lost Generation.* New York: Macmillan, 1951.

————. *The Devil in the Fire: Retrospective Essays on American Literature and Culture, 1951–1971.* New York: Harper's Magazine Press, 1972.

————. *Time to Murder and Create: The Contemporary Novel in Crisis.* New York: McKay, 1966.

Balakian, Nona, and Charles Simmons, eds. *The Creative Present: Notes on Contemporary American Fiction.* New York: Doubleday, 1963.

Baumbach, Jonathan. *The Landscape of Nightmare: Studies in the Contemporary American Novel.* New York: New York University Press, 1965.

Blotner, Joseph. *The Modern American Political Novel, 1900–1960.* Austin: The University of Texas Press, 1966.

Bone, Robert A. *The Negro Novel in America.* New Haven: Yale University Press, 1958.

Bryant, Jerry H. *The Open Decision: The Contemporary American Novel and Its Intellectual Background.* New York: The Free Press, 1970.

Eisinger, Chester E. *Fiction of the Forties.* Chicago: University of Chicago Press, 1963.

Fiedler, Leslie. *No! In Thunder.* Boston: Beacon Press, 1960.

————. *Waiting for the End.* New York: Stein and Day, 1964.

Galloway, David. *The Absurd Hero in American Fiction.* Austin: University of Texas Press, 1966.

Geismar, Maxwell. *American Moderns: A Mid-Century View of Contemporary Fiction.* New York: Hill and Wang, 1958.

Gossett, Louise Y. *Violence in Recent Southern Fiction.* Durham: Duke University Press, 1965.

Harper, Howard M., Jr. *Desperate Faith: A Study of Bellow, Salinger, Mailer, Baldwin, and Updike.* Chapel Hill: University of North Carolina Press, 1967.

Hassan, Ihab. *Radical Innocence: The Contemporary American Novel.* Princeton, N. J.: Princeton University Press, 1961.

Hicks, Granville. *The Living Novel: A Symposium.* New York: Macmillan, 1957.

Hill, Herbert, ed. *Anger and Beyond: The Negro Writer in the United States.* New York: Harper & Row, 1966.

Hoffman, Frederick J. *The Art of Southern Fiction: A Study of Some Modern Novelists.* Carbondale: University of Southern Illinois Press, 1967.

Kazin, Alfred. *Contemporaries.* Boston: Atlantic, Little, Brown, 1962.

Klein, Marcus. *After Alienation: American Novels in Mid-Century.* Cleveland: World Publishing Company, 1964.

Klein, Marcus, ed. *The American Novel Since World War II.* Greenwich, Conn.: Fawcett, 1969.

Kostelanetz, Richard, ed. *On Contemporary Literature.* New York: Avon, 1964.

Ludwig, Jack. *Recent American Novelists.* Minneapolis: University of Minneosta Press, 1962.

Malin, Irving. *Jews and Americans.* Carbondale: University of Southern Illinois Press, 1965.

————. *New American Gothic.* Carbondale: University of Southern Illinois Press, 1962.

Nevius, Blake. *The American Novel: Sinclair Lewis to the Present.* New York: Appleton-Century-Crofts, 1970.

Olderman, Raymond M. *Beyond the Waste Land: The American Novel in the Nineteen-sixties.* New Haven: Yale University Press, 1972.

Podhoretz, Norman. *Doings and Undoings: The Fifties and After in American Writing.* New York: Farrar, Straus & Giroux, 1964.

Rubin, Louis D., Jr. *The Faraway Country: Writers of the Modern South.* Seattle: University of Washington Press, 1963.

Rupp, Richard H. *Celebration in Postwar American Fiction.* Coral Gables, Florida: University of Miami Press, 1970.

Scholes, Robert. *The Fabulators*. New York: Oxford University Press, 1967.

Schultz, Max F. *Radical Sophistication*. Athens: Ohio University Press, 1969.

Scott, Nathan A., Jr., ed. *Adversity and Grace: Studies in Recent American Literature*. Chicago: University of Chicago Press, 1968.

Tanner, Tony. *City of Words: American Fiction, 1950–1970*. New York: Harper and Row, 1971.

Waldmeir, Joseph J., ed. *Recent American Fiction: Some Critical Views*. Boston: Houghton, Mifflin, 1963.

Weinberg, Helen A. *The New Novel in America: The Kafkan Mode in Contemporary Fiction*. Ithaca, N. Y.: Cornell University Press, 1971.

Contemporary Poetry

Alvarez, A. *Beyond All This Fiddle*. London: Allen Lane, 1968.

Cambon, Galuco. *Recent American Poetry*. Minneapolis: University of Minnesota Press, 1963.

Carroll, Paul. *The Poem in Its Skin*. Chicago: Follett, 1968.

Dickey, James, ed. *From Babel to Byzantium: Poets and Poetry Now*. New York: Farrar, Straus & Giroux, 1968.

Dodsworth, Martin, ed. *The Survival of Poetry*. London: Faber, 1970.

Fiedler, Leslie. *Waiting for the End*. New York: Stein and Day, 1964.

Hamilton, Ian, ed. *The Modern Poet*. London: Macdonald, 1969.

Howard, Richard. *Alone With America*. New York: Athenaeum, 1969.

Hungerford, Edward B., ed. *Poets in Progress: Critical Prefaces to Ten Contemporary Americans*. Evanston, Ill.: Northwestern University Press, 1962.

Jarrell, Randall. *Poetry and the Age*. New York: Knopf, 1955.

Mills, Ralf J., Jr. *Contemporary American Poetry*. New York: Random House, 1965.

Nemerov, Howard. *Reflexions on Poetry and Poetics*. New Brunswick, N. J.: Rutgers University Press, 1972.

Nemerov, Howard, ed. *Poets on Poetry*. New York: Basic Books, 1966.

Ossman, David. *The Sullen Art*. New York: Corinth Books, 1963.

Ostroff, Anthony, ed. *The Contemporary Poet as Artist and Critic*. Boston: Little, Brown, 1964.

Ransom, John Crowe et al. *American Poetry at Mid-Century*. Washington: Library of Congress, 1958.

Rosenthal, M. L. *The New Poets*. New York: Oxford University Press, 1967.

Stepanchev, Stephen. *American Poetry Since 1945*. New York: Harper & Row, 1965.

Contemporary Drama

Atkinson, J. Brooks. *Broadway Scrapbook*. New York: Theatre Arts, 1947.

Bigsby, C. W. E. *Confrontation and Commitment: A Study of Contemporary American Drama, 1959–1966*. Kansas City: University of Missouri Press, 1968.

Blau, Herbert. *The Impossible Theater*. New York: Macmillan, 1964.

Broussard, Louis. *American Drama: Contemporary Allegory from Eugene O'Neill to Tennessee Williams*. Norman: University of Oklahoma Press, 1962.

Brustein, Robert. *The Third Theatre*. New York: Knopf, 1969.

Clurman, Harold. *The Naked Image: Observations in the Modern Theatre*. New York: Macmillan, 1966.

Driver, Tom F. *Romantic Quest and Modern Query: A History of the Modern Theatre*. New York: Delacorte Press, 1970.

Downer, Alan S. *Recent American Drama*. Minneapolis: University of Minnesota Press, 1961.

Gardner, R. H. *The Splintered Stage: The Decline of the American Theatre*. New York: Macmillan, 1965.

Gassner, John. *The Theatre in Our Time*. New York: Dryden, 1954.

Gilman, Richard. *Common and Uncommon Masks: Writings on Theatre, 1961–1970.* New York: Random House, 1971.

Gottfried, Martin. *A Theater Divided: The Postwar American Stage.* Boston: Little, Brown, 1968.

Gould, Jean. *Modern American Playwrights.* New York: Dodd, Mead, 1966.

Lewis, Allan. *American Plays and Playwrights of the Contemporary Theatre.* Rev. ed. New York: Crown, 1970.

McCarthy, Mary. *Theatre Chronicles, 1937–1962.* New York: Farrar, Straus & Giroux, 1963.

Mitchell, Loften. *Black Drama: The Story of the American Negro in the Theatre.* New York: Hawthorn, 1967.

Nathan, George Jean. *The Theatre in the Fifties.* New York: Knopf, 1953.

Novick, Julius. *Beyond Broadway: The Quest for Permanent Theatres.* New York: Hill & Wang, 1968.

Price, Julia. *The Off-Broadway Theatre.* New York: Scarecrow Press, 1962.

Sievers, W. David. *Freud on Broadway: A History of Psychoanalysis and the American Drama.* New York: Hermitage House, 1955.

Schechner, Richard. *Public Domain.* New York: Bobbs Merrill, 1969.

Schevill, James. *Breakout: In Search of New Theatrical Environments.* Chicago: Swallow Press, 1973.

Weales, Gerald. *American Drama since World War II.* New York: Harcourt, Brace, 1961.

———. *The Jumping-Off Place: American Drama in the 1960's.* New York: Macmillan, 1969.

INDEX OF AUTHORS